E S S E N T I A L

BMW ROADSTERS
& CABRIOLETS

ESSENTIAL
BMW ROADSTERS
& CABRIOLETS

THE CARS AND THEIR STORY FROM 328 TO Z3

EBERHARD KITTLER

Published 1996 by Bay View Books Ltd
The Red House, 25-26 Bridgeland Street,
Bideford, Devon EX39 2PZ, UK

© Copyright 1996 by Bay View Books Ltd
Translated by Anders Ditlev Clausager
Edited by Mark Hughes
Typesetting and design by Chris Fayers & Sarah Ward

ISBN 1 870979 77 X
Printed in Hong Kong

CONTENTS

SIX APPEAL

The B in BMW stands for Bavaria and the marque may be synonymous with Munich, yet many famous BMWs have come from other cities, nowadays even from other countries: the world-beating Z3 is made exclusively at Spartanburg, South Carolina, in the USA. More than 60 years ago, the 'Bavarian' BMW came not from Bavaria but from Thuringia. In 1928, BMW had taken over the old-established 'Fahrzeugfabrik' in Eisenach, almost 200 miles (300km) from Munich. This was the home of the Dixi, the German licence-built version of the Austin Seven which despite its undoubted qualities failed to safeguard the independence of its depression-hit German maker.

The course that BMW took in 1928 would be repeated almost 40 years later when it took over the Glas company of Dingolfing. The original factory was kept going after the take-over and so was the car produced at

6

The ancestor: the 3/15hp Wartburg Sport, type DA3, hailed from the factory at Eisenach, just like all other pre-war BMWs. Until taken over by BMW, the Eisenach company had built the Austin Seven under licence.

The BMW 315/1, a lightweight sports car at only 1652lb (750kg), captured the hearts of enthusiasts young and old. With its long bonnet, cut-away doors and tapering rear end, it became the pattern for all later roadsters.

the factory – but the product was measurably improved and given the seal of approval in the form of the blue and white BMW roundel. Until 1928 BMW had only made aero engines and motorcycles. The company was a late comer to the world of car manufacture, and the early Dixis were very modest compared with the legendary sports cars which ten short years later would earn world-wide fame. Even so there are those who claim that BMW could only afford to build cars in the 1930s because it made so much money from its aero engines!

Still, BMW had a good idea of what to do when it came to cars. For the first few years after taking over Dixi, the original 3/15hp four-cylinder car formed the staple production model – if in an increasing number of variations. Among these was the Wartburg sports roadster, Dixi model DA3, of which only 150 were made. It featured a more streamlined boat-tail body and the engine was tuned to all of 18bhp. Modest though this was, it was still sufficient for the Wartburg to make an impression in the 1-litre class in motor racing. Weighing a fraction over 900lb (410kg), the little car would (eventually) reach a top speed of 62mph (100kph). If you had the patience, the car had the speed! By contrast, MG at the time was building far more powerful small sports

cars with single overhead camshaft engines where the Dixi had to make do with side valves. The British cars with the octagon badge became benchmarks for BMW.

In those depression years, many car manufacturers went under, and of the survivors many were forced to merge with competitors – such as the famous German companies Daimler and Benz, or the four companies from Saxony which got together to form Auto Union in 1932. BMW had to take care to avoid a similar fate! Only in 1932, when BMW had reached a modest but healthy 5% share of the German market, did the company deem that the time was ripe for a new model. This was the AM1, designed in Munich by Max Friz, who was the father of the BMW flat-twin shaft-drive motorcycle. At the time the AM1 3/20hp model was introduced, BMW cancelled the licence agreement with Austin. Sadly, although the AM1 had an advanced paper specification with its backbone type chassis and all–independent suspension, it was afflicted with poor handling and steering, but its new 788cc overhead valve four-cylinder engine was a portent of things to come.

BMW's managing director, Franz-Joseph Popp (whose daughter Erika was later to marry the British racing driver Richard Seaman), had ambitious plans for a

six-cylinder car. He wanted to see BMW become a leader in car manufacture, just as the company was leading in the aero engine field. The less than satisfactory AM1 would be replaced by a new car, with a new chassis of tubular construction designed by the team at Eisenach. Design engineer Rudolf Schleicher was recruited from Horch to turn Popp's ambition into reality. Schleicher had a simple prescription: take the existing four-cylinder overhead valve engine, add another two cylinders and replace the single carburettor with two. It is amusing to relate that BMW sought the advice of Hans Nibel, then chief designer at Mercedes-Benz, and he was happy to endorse the new six-cylinder as a simple, economical but clever solution.

The 303 was thus the first BMW car to be fitted with a six-cylinder engine. This was an unusually small unit, well below the normal 2-litre limit for sixes, with a capacity of barely 1.2 litres. However, there were comparable power units in Britain: the Morris/ Wolseley/MG group followed a path similar to BMW, taking the four-cylinder engine from the Morris Minor and MG Midget and creating the small 'six' which saw service in the Wolseley Hornet and MG Magna. In the case of BMW, the bore and stroke (56×80mm) of the original four-cylinder engine were unchanged, resulting in a displacement of 1182cc. The overhead valves were the same, the camshaft offered the same valve timing, and with two Solex 26 carburettors the new engine developed 30bhp at 4000rpm.

The chassis for the new 303 six-cylinder model was far more conventional than the backbone of the AM1. The 303 had a 'proper' chassis with tubular side members

and box-section crossmembers, giving the frame great torsional rigidity. Independent front suspension was by transverse leaf spring and lower wishbones, while the live rear axle had semi-elliptic springs. The chassis – indeed, the complete car – was commendably low in weight, a characteristic of many BMW cars yet to come.

The new BMW made its debut in February 1933 at the International Motor Show in Berlin – the first to be opened by Germany's new Führer, Adolf Hitler. For the first time a BMW car appeared with the famous 'double kidney' radiator grille, although this was not actually a BMW idea. The inspiration came from the small coachbuilder, Ihle, of Bruchsal in Baden: this company had turned out special-bodied Dixis with this type of radiator and also offered similar radiators on its special-bodied DKWs. The prototype 303 roadster on the BMW stand in 1933 had its headlamps inset at the top of the radiator, but when the cars went into production later in the year the headlamps were conventionally mounted between the radiator and the wings.

Around the time that the 303 went into production in the early summer of 1933, the company recruited a new designer, Fritz Fiedler (1899-1972), who followed in Schleicher's footsteps by moving from Horch to BMW. At Horch he had designed a new generation of luxury straight-eights, but he may have become uncertain of the future after Horch was merged into the new Auto Union conglomerate. He now assumed responsibility as chief designer for the very different small BMWs, and for more than 30 years would put his stamp on all the company's products. His first project became the 309, in effect a version of the 303 with a four-cylinder engine developed from the AM1, and the last four-cylinder car from BMW until the 1960s. He also took the 303 under his wing and set about developing a bigger six-cylinder car.

The result was the 315, which appeared in 1934 and could hardly be distinguished externally from the 303. BMW type numbers now acquired a degree of logic – the 309 had a 900 engine (to be exact, 845cc) while the 315 had a 1500 engine (1490cc), achieved by enlarging the dimensions of the 'six' to 58×94mm. Retaining the four main bearing crankshaft, this engine had an output of 34bhp. The standard model reached an easy 63mph (100kph), and a two-door saloon cost 3750 Reichsmark. For another RM 1000 there was a two-seater roadster (or 'Sport Cabriolet') on the same chassis. This had an attractive body with a flowing line from the front wing into the running board, deep elbow cut-outs in the doors and removable sidescreens.

More interesting still was the 315/1, a tuned version of the two-seater. With higher compression and three Solex 26 carburettors, this developed 40bhp at 4300rpm, and reached a top speed of almost 78mph (125kph). The petrol tank, still under the bonnet, was enlarged to 11 gallons (50 litres), and the car could be fitted with a higher rear axle ratio of 4.5:1 instead of the standard ratio of 5.15:1. The 315/1 was usually seen with rear wheel spats, and was available with centre-lock wire wheels. The price for all this was RM 5200.

Worthy sports car though the 315/1 was, to achieve real credibility BMW would have to make a 2-litre car to be competitive in what was at the time the most important class in sports car racing. It seems to have been a simple matter to enlarge the six-cylinder engine yet again, this time to 65×96mm and 1911cc. The result was the 319 range, introduced at the Berlin Motor Show in 1935. The 315 and 319 models shared many of the same body styles and looked almost identical, and the 1.5-litre model remained in production. The sports model of the 319 was called the 319/1, again very similar to the 315/1, but with still higher compression of 6.8:1, larger Solex 30 carburettors, and 55bhp at 4000rpm. With a low weight of just over 1700lb (780kg), a top speed of 84mph (135kph) became possible – spectacular for the time. At RM 5800, the 319/1 was RM 600 more expensive than the 315/1 – a modest increase, yet at the time the equivalent of four months' pay for a worker in German industry…

From now on, the 315/1 and 319/1 became serious competitors in motor racing throughout most of Europe. In particular there was the 2000km German Trial of 1934, a tough non-stop event which was just as hard on the cars as the more famous Mille Miglia. But the two-seaters from the BMW works team came through with flying colours and were awarded a gold medal. Further BMW honours came in the International Alpine Rally of the same year. The BMWs attracted notice in the 1935 Monte Carlo Rally, and in the Austrian Alpine Trial which ran from Nice to Munich in 1935 the works cars won their class and the team award. Ernst von Delius took his 319/1 to a win in the unsupercharged 2-litre class in the *Eifelrennen*, and further successes came in the *Kesselbergrennen*, the 1000-mile run in Czechoslovakia, the *Feldbergrennen*, the Austrian International Mountain trials and the International Reliability Trial from Lake Constance (Germany/Switzerland) to Lake Balaton (Hungary) in 1936. In 1937, Louise Leander's BMW won the hillclimb at Rio Petropolis in Brazil, and a 315/1 was the overall winner of the Balkan Rally in Athens. Ralph Roese in a 315/1 was the German motor

In the Eifel race at the Nürburgring (below) in the summer of 1935, the BMW 315/1 roadster competed against such cars as this Fiat Ballila **sports car. Running for a class win (below right): a 319/1 at Athens, during the 1937 Balkan Rally. This rally car was largely to standard specification.**

A right-hand drive Frazer Nash-BMW 319/1, originally sold in Britain

A Frazer Nash-BMW, a 1936 319 with British drophead coupé body.

racing champion of 1939 in the 1.5-litre class. Even in Britain the small BMWs had a following, challenging local opposition in club events, trials and hillclimbs.

There was a certain irony in the fact that BMW's first car, the Dixi, had been a British car built under licence – namely the Austin Seven – but the new generation of all-German BMWs returned the favour by being adopted by a British car manufacturer, as the Frazer Nash-BMW. H.J. Aldington, the managing director of Frazer Nash, had taken part in one of his chain-drive sports cars in the 1934 Alpine Trial and had been greatly impressed by the performance of the BMWs. He wrote to the company in Munich and in November 1934 was awarded a contract which gave Frazer Nash the exclusive rights to selling BMW cars in the UK and the British empire, where they would be called Frazer Nash-BMW. Although Aldington had talked of actually manufacturing BMW cars under licence in England, these plans never came to fruition despite some discussions with the Riley company in Coventry. Instead, the cars were imported from Eisenach – a few early ones had left-hand drive but BMW soon began to fit right-hand drive. BMW also shipped many cars in chassis form for Frazer Nash to have fitted with British-built coachwork, but the sports models were mostly imported complete.

The new Frazer Nash-BMW cars were so popular in

Britain that they all but ousted the original chain-drive sports cars – but not before one or two of the 'real Nashes' had been fitted with BMW engines! Britain very quickly became the most important export market for BMW, and the Aldingtons developed close personal ties with BMW's management. Indeed, it is said that BMW's largest pre-war model, the 3.5-litre 335, was developed with an eye to the British market, and it was launched in Britain at the 1938 Earls Court Motor Show. While this car was not offered as a sports model, it was naturally available with convertible bodywork.

Meanwhile, the new BMW 329 was introduced in 1936. This was a development of the 315/319 range, with more or less the same chassis and the same 2 litre

There is timeless beauty in the design of the BMW 327, whether in coupé or convertible form – but these cars brought BMW little, if any, profit.

The BMW 326 had a longer wheelbase and a more up-to-date shape, and brought more converts into the BMW fold. The four-window cabriolet was particularly sought-after.

engine, but it had larger, roomier bodywork and the lines were brought up to date with a hint of the contemporary streamlining. It was, however, available only in four-seater convertible form and was not a real sports car. Much more important was the 326 model, which was the sensation of the 1936 Berlin Motor Show. The 326 was built on a new long-wheelbase box-section chassis, and its six-cylinder engine, with a 66mm bore and 1971cc, gave 50bhp at 3750rpm. The brakes were hydraulic and there was new rear suspension by torsion bars. For the first time, a BMW was available with a four-door saloon or convertible body. But the 326 was not intended as a sports car, nor were the later 320 and 321 models, which were basically short-wheelbase versions with two-door coachwork. They did not inherit the mantle of the 315/1 and the 319/1, which went out of production in 1936 after a total production of 408 cars.

The best, however, was yet to come. BMW was developing the ultimate 80bhp version of the pre-war 1971cc six-cylinder engine. It was to be fitted to the most legendary and fastest of all pre-war BMWs – the

With the 335, here in four-door cabriolet form, BMW entered the real prestige sector of the car market. The six-cylinder engine was enlarged to 3.5 litres and developed 90bhp.

328. Even the beautiful 327, developed from the 326, had to give best to the 328. Although the BMW customer at the time was spoiled for choice, it is likely that such a wide range of delectable models brought BMW more fame than profit. Of the two, it was the 327 that was resurrected after the war, and although still made in Eisenach it was known as the EMW and carried a red and white badge as a symbol of the new political order in what had then become East Germany.

THE ICON: 328

It must be admitted that the sports car was not a German – or Bavarian – invention. The concept of the uncompromising open two-seater with cramped cockpit and inadequate weather protection came from Britain. However impractical, the British sports car had a special appeal to enthusiasts all over the world, and for a long time cars like the classic MGs or the Jaguar SS 100 have been icons. Evidently non-British manufacturers saw these cars as worth imitating.

Delighting the eye, the BMW 328 held true to sports car traditions: there was no superfluous equipment, not even bumpers.

With the 315/1 BMW had clearly taken up the sports car challenge and created its own niche in the market. BMW considered that there was no better form of advertising than success in motor sport, and so it began to build fast, but affordable, two-seaters. The target group

Powerful heart. Although still with a conventional side camshaft, the 328's 2-litre six-cylinder engine had a brilliantly conceived valve design which helped it to develop a remarkable 80bhp. The three carburettors, however, were not easy to adjust!

was middle-class customers, young or young at heart, male or female – in old advertising photos a woman driver is often seen at the wheel of a sporting BMW. Of course only the middle class could afford cars in those days; a worker on average pay could not afford any kind of car, much less a BMW sports car, and only aspired to a motorcycle at most.

Following by now well-established design principles, and using mostly off-the-shelf components from more sedate models, the BMW sports cars developed apace. Even that first effort, the 315/1, had plenty in reserve as regards performance and handling. Year after year there were new surprises from BMW, dreamed up by chief designer Fiedler with assistance from Schleicher, who combined the functions of chief tester and works team manager. They pulled off their biggest coup on 14 June 1936 when they revealed the brand new 328. The occasion was the *Eifelrennen* at the Nürburgring, where the prototype 328 (production cars came six months later) was driven by Ernst Henne, who also held the motorcycle land speed record for BMW. He fended off all the competition and led from start to finish.

The new two–seater roadster was quite as basic and spartan as the enthusiasts expected. Those in search of greater comfort could apply to specialist coachbuilders,

which did not bother BMW in the slightest: the company ended up selling more than ten per cent of 328 production in chassis form. The basis of the car was the traditional tubular frame, as light and rigid as ever, the side members being thin-walled tubes of 90mm diameter, held together by three welded-in crossmembers – this design had proved itself on the 315/1 and 319/1. The bodywork of the new car was mostly in steel, but aluminium was used for the bonnet, doors and tail panel. Greater use of this expensive material would have made the car even more expensive than the RM 7400 ticket on a complete car (the chassis only cost RM 5900). In fact the 328 was priced about RM 1000 higher than the Mercedes-Benz 230 two-seater. In Britain a 328 cost £695, against the £395 asked for the 2½-litre SS 100 or £445 for the 3½-litre version.

The 328's styling followed the 326 saloon model, the front ends being very similar, but the two-seater had cut-down doors and no external handles, and the narrow running boards were extensions of the front wings. While most other BMW models had bodies supplied by Ambi-Budd in Berlin (the German equivalent of the Pressed Steel company) or other specialists, the 328 was completely built in the factory at Eisenach. After some delay sales began in February 1937.

The white 328 was supplied without rear wheel spats, but they were fitted to the red car. The well-rounded rear sports the spare wheel slightly inset, and a large petrol filler.

This 328 is a welcome guest at the Mille Miglia – and the number plate is as special as the car.

Although the 328 had the same wheelbase and track as its 315/1 and 319/1 predecessors, the new car was 4in (100mm) longer and also wider. Yet it appeared more compact, and the body seemed to fit more tightly round the mechanical components. The bonnet was longer, with the narrow radiator grille pushed further forward. It was a more modern looking car, with rounder, more flowing lines and headlamps built into the wings. On the other hand, the spare wheel was now carried out of doors, set into the tail panel. Of bumpers there were none. The contemporary catchphrase was 'streamlining', and while the proper science of aerodynamics was increasingly practised in Germany, with many of the pioneers choosing to build their experimental bodies on BMW chassis, the normal 328 body was developed by BMW's own team under Fiedler's guidance. But it was not developed in a wind tunnel: in any case such work was typically only possible with fifth-scale models. If drag was one enemy, weight was the other, and here the 328 scored well as it tipped the scales at only 1828lb (830kg).

Under the strapped-down bonnet sat the best feature of the car: the engine. One might have expected an all-new design, perhaps with one or two overhead camshafts, but BMW's engine designers had, if anything, been more clever than that. Presumably to keep costs down, they had done an outstanding job of modifying the basic 2-litre six-cylinder engine from the 326. The strong bottom end was kept but an all-new cylinder head was developed, with the valves in V-configuration. To keep the camshaft in its conventional position in the block, the inlet valves were operated by long pushrods and short rocker arms, and to get around the difficulty of operating the exhaust valves on the other side of the engine, BMW developed cross-pushrods operated by the rocker shaft on the inlet side, running across the valley formed by the two rocker covers and operating the exhaust valve rocker arms in turn. The inlet tracts were almost vertical, descending from the top of the engine, which was crowned by three Solex 30 downdraught carburettors with small individual air cleaners. The end result was an engine which in all respects was comparable with more complicated and costlier overhead camshaft designs.

Made from cast aluminium, the cylinder head had hemispherical combustion chambers. These had already featured on the 315/1 but without the vertical inlet tracts of the new engine. The three-carburettor set-up had also been found on the earlier cars but only with the simpler

Even today, the 328 offers a remarkable driving experience – this is one of the finest sports cars ever.

In keeping with its competition heritage, the 328 remains a popular choice in historic races for pre-war sports cars.

side-draught Solexes. New on the 328 was an oil cooler fitted in front of the radiator. The compression ratio of 7.5:1 was very high for the 1930s – the 'cooking' 326 engine had a 6:1 ratio. Despite the long 96mm stroke, the 328 engine proved to be capable of high revs and 5000rpm was possible from the start, later engines being capable of up to 6000rpm. Even more surprising was the fact that racing versions proved able to stand up to further tuning. In standard form the 328 engine gave 80bhp, and the car had an unequalled power-to-weight ratio – less than 23lb (10.3kg) per bhp. A top speed of 93mph (150kph) was well within reach, while race-prepared cars were quicker still, particularly those with aerodynamic bodywork.

The designers of the 328 deliberately avoided complicated or expensive solutions. Thus the suspension was adapted from the 319/1 and retained leaf springs –

a transverse spring for the independent front suspension and semi-elliptics for the live rear axle. The shock absorbers were hydraulic. One important improvement was that the mechanical brakes of the 319/1 were replaced by hydraulic brakes, with bigger drums, up from 240 to 280mm. On the other hand, the original ZF gearbox, a four-speeder with synchromesh on third and top, was not up to coping with the powerful engine. It was soon replaced by a Hurth 'box and the final drive ratio was lowered from 3.7 to 3.88:1. The standard type of wheel was a 16in disc with five-bolt fixing, while centre-lock disc wheels were optional. The rear-mounted petrol tank held 11 gallons (50 litres) but another option was a 22 gallon (100 litre) tank.

Between 1936-40 BMW built precisely 461 examples of the 328. Forty-two of these were sold in Britain and Frazer Nash-BMW also accounted for two overseas deliveries (to India and the USA). Of exports to the UK, seven were in chassis form, of which six were only completed after the war. Total chassis deliveries from Eisenach amounted to 59 cars, most being fitted with bodies by German coachbuilders including Gläser in Dresden and Drauz in Heilbronn. They were mostly convertibles or drophead coupés, including at least six cars bodied by Authenrieth in Darmstadt. Wendler of Reutlingen built similar drophead coupés but also constructed two streamlined coupés designed by the German pioneer of aerodynamics, Freiherr Koenig-Fachsenfeld. These cars had a drag coefficient of 0.382. Further dropheads were built in Munich, by the

Vereinigte Werkstätten and by Ludwig Weinberger, who also created a one-off special roadster allegedly inspired by American designs. The racing driver Ralph Roese concocted his own monstrous special, which was roughly cigar-shaped.

The 328 and its relations ....

One other BMW model enjoyed the benefits of the powerful 80bhp 328 engine – the beautiful 327 coupé and convertible models. Introduced in November 1937 on an intermediate wheelbase (shorter than 326, longer than 328 and in fact shared with the 'cooking' two-door 320), the 327 had a 326 engine slightly tuned to 55bhp, and was originally available as a two-door, two-plus-two convertible – a GT car of the 1930s. After one year, a fixed-head coupé was introduced and both versions were now offered with the 80bhp engine as an alternative, becoming the 327/28 models (also sometimes called the 327/80, where the normal model was the 327/55). BMW made 1396 of the standard 327s and 569 of the 327/28s, which at RM 8100 were the most expensive of all the 2-litre models. In one sense, the 327/28 anticipated BMW's M-models which came more than 50 years later.

Some 328s were re-bodied in the post-war period. In particular, the Swiss coachbuilders Graber and Beutler built convertibles which, in contemporary fashion, had rather smoother bodywork than the original. Back home in Germany the Veritas company at Messkirch in Baden built a series of cars derived from the 328, using such stocks of BMW parts as it could obtain. Heading this enterprise was Ernst Loof, former motorcycle racer and BMW racing manager. He joined forces with businessman Lorenz Dietrich and another motorcycle ace, Georg 'Schorsch' Meier. Between them they managed to build 62 cars, fitted with open or closed bodies, usually constructed from aluminium. Many of them were built for racing, and among the drivers who took to the Veritas was Karl Kling, later a member of the Mercedes-Benz racing team. In the early post-war period these Veritas racers were extremely successful but the company made no money and, inevitably, Veritas went out of business.

There were also the AFM cars, equally successful in racing and the brainchild of Alexander von Falkenhausen – an engineer who had worked in the BMW racing department before the war. AFM drivers included Hans Stuck, who had gained fame at the wheel of the Auto Union Grand Prix cars in the pre-war era of the 'Silver Arrows', and Hermann Lang and Manfred von Brauchitsch, once of the Mercedes-Benz team.

Even outside Germany the 328 would come back with a vengeance after the war, and would survive until the end of the 1950s. This was due to H.J. Aldington and Frazer Nash. In 1945, Aldington and his brother W.H. managed to get to Munich a matter of months after the German capitulation. They returned with some excess baggage – one of the special-bodied 328s that had run in the 1940 Mille Miglia. Soon after, Frazer Nash presented its first post-war model, which was simply the old 328 masquerading behind another radiator grille! The Aldingtons also persuaded Fritz Fiedler to join them in England for a time; Fiedler had worked on armaments in Germany during the war and was therefore temporarily *persona non grata* with the allied control commission, and not allowed to work in Germany. The actual production models which followed from Frazer Nash from 1947 used much-developed versions of the BMW engine, now putting out some 125bhp and reaching a top speed close to 125mph (200kph). A Frazer Nash 'High Speed' model was third in the 1949 Le Mans – hence the famous 'Le Mans Replica' – and in 1951 a similar car was the first British car to win the Targa Florio.

Aldington had another string to his bow: the joint project with the aircraft manufacturer Bristol to develop a touring car. The result was the Bristol 400, which in all respects was based on BMW practice – chassis, engine, and a body that bore more than a passing resemblance to the 327. It was, however, a very expensive car at £2375, more than twice a Jaguar XK120. The 400 was soon replaced by the 401 with an aerodynamic body using Touring *Superleggera* construction under licence – the styling was not everybody's cup of tea and at £2460 it was hardly for 'everyman' anyway. Later Bristols became known as the 'businessman's express'. Bristol engines were originally of 2 litres and developed 100bhp, while later models had more powerful 2.2-litre units. These BMW-derived engines survived until the early 1960s and were then replaced by Chrysler V8 engines.

A side issue was the American-sponsored Arnolt-Bristol Bolide. With its spartan Bertone-built open two-seater body, this was perhaps the post-war car that best evoked the original 328 concept. Bristol also at one time supplied engines to the AC company, for use in the Aceca and Greyhound models, apart from the most famous of them all, the AC Ace, which was a direct forerunner of the Cobra. The Bristol-engined ACs typically had around 130bhp – further proof of the considerable potential of the original 1936 design.

Three special-bodied 328s. A cabrio (above) from Weinberger in Munich, with higher doors and well-padded soft-top. One of two aerodynamic coupés (above right) built by Wendler in Reutlingen, and able to reach 112mph. This full-width body on a 328 chassis (right) is by Swiss coachbuilder Beutler, of Thun near Bern.

The 328 in racing ....

The 328 began as it meant to continue. The three prototypes revealed at the *Eifelrennen* in June 1936 were very similar to the production models that followed, although they had doorless bodies. Their maximum output was around 90bhp, achieved with the help of a carefully balanced crankshaft, while they also featured aluminium brake drums and the long-distance 22-gallon petrol tanks. Of the three works drivers, class winner Ernst Henne was the most notable, mainly for his exploits on two wheels. Between 1929–37 he set no fewer than

76 speed records on BMW bikes, his 1937 record of almost 174mph (280kph) remaining unbeaten for 20 years. Henne was also a BMW dealer and at 32 years of age not exactly a novice on four wheels, having been one of the first drivers chosen for the new Mercedes–Benz Grand Prix team in 1934.

It was a brilliant debut for the new sports car. It was, so to speak, a *formule libre* handicap race where 1½-litre racing cars started against sports cars, with blown or unblown engines, the single-seaters having a two minute head start. Henne in the works 328 took the lead in the sports car class, pushing a privately entered blown Alfa

17

Ernst Loof, who later designed the forerunner of the 507, was the brains behind the Veritas, although this company was ultimately unsuccessful. Meteor (left) and R1 (below left) versions were seen.

This Volpini racer, built in 1947 on a 328 chassis, looks very much like a Veritas.

Romeo into second place, and kept well up with the single-seaters. With a race average of 63mph (101.5kph) he was the hero of the hour, and the 328 had made its mark. Apart from not having any doors, these cars also lacked the external spare wheel on the tail panel, and were fitted with low one-piece racing windscreens. Other details also differed from the later production models.

The next 328 experience was a less happy occasion. In the French Grand Prix, held for sports cars at Montlhéry in June 1936, all three 328 prototypes retired. Better luck was to be had in the Tourist Trophy, run over the Ards circuit at Belfast in September 1936. Here the works cars were painted British Racing Green in honour of the occasion and one by now had right-hand drive (yet they still sported the Munich number plates!). Two of the drivers this time were British, H.J. Aldington

and A.F.P. Fane, and Thai Prince Bira was the third. Fane finished third overall and the Frazer Nash-BMW cars took the team award.

The following year, 1937, saw the 328s dominate most of the important international sports car races. In the Tourist Trophy, this time held at Donington Park, Bira won the 2-litre class and finished third overall. S.C.H. 'Sammy' Davis, sports editor of *The Autocar* and former Bentley boy, took the prototype 328 (chassis number 87,003) to Brooklands and put 103.227 miles into a one-hour demonstration run. At the Nürburgring Fane set a new class lap record in the *Eifelrennen*, and another BMW victory was scored in the Bucharest Grand Prix. However, the performance of an aerodynamic Jaray-designed Adler coupé in the Le Mans 24 Hours was an incentive for BMW to raise its sights to sports car racing at the highest level.

Racing 328s in standard-bodied form. A successful team effort in the 1936 Tourist Trophy over the Ards circuit (right), with drivers Fane (18), Bira (17) and Aldington (19). Bira duelling with a Riley (below) in the 1937 TT at Donington Park. An early one-model race (bottom) held at the Nürburgring in 1938; the winner was Paul Greifzu (10) at an average of almost 70mph.

One of the three
roadsters with works
bodies built for BMW's
successful run in the
'Ersatz' Mille Miglia of
1940.

Sisters under the
(aluminium) skin:
standard 328 and works-
bodied Mille Miglia
roadster.

In 1938, therefore, BMW for the first time contested the Mille Miglia, at the time the most important sports car road race of all. Undoubtedly the hot favourites were the blood-red Alfa Romeos, the blown 6C 2300 models with around 300bhp. The four white BMWs started in the less prominent class for unblown sports cars. There were three works cars, driven by Prince Max Zu Schaumburg-Lippe/Count Giovanni Lurani, Fane/Bill James and Ulrich Richter/Fritz Werneck, plus the private entry of Heinrich Graf von der Mühle-Eckart and Theo Holzschuh. The results were noteworthy. The BMWs finished 1-2-3-4 in their class, the best overall placing

eighth for Fane/James, with the others 10th, 11th and 12th. The highest-placed car finished at an average of almost 75mph (120kph).

In the summer of that year, as part of the German Grand Prix meeting at the Nürburgring, there was a special sports car 'grand prix' race contested solely by 328s. The winner was Paul Greifzu, who improved on Fane's lap record from the previous year. Other 328 victories came in the 24-hour race at Spa-Francorchamps in Belgium, and in the Shelsley Walsh hillclimb. It was no great surprise when the 328 became the German hillclimb champion for 1938.

The aerodynamic efficiency of the Touring-built coupé, winner of the 1940 Mille Miglia, gave it a top speed of 150mph – and this recent wind tunnel evaluation established its drag coefficient at 0.26.

The focus of attention shifted to North Africa in early 1939. In the Tobruk-Benghazi-Tripolis road race in Libya, Alfa Romeo was again the winner but the three BMW works cars finished well, with third place for Wilhelm Briem/Theo Holzschuh, with their team-mates fifth and sixth. At the end of the season Helmut Polensky in a 328 became the German racing champion in the 2-litre class. Also in 1939, the Romanian driver Cristea set a new class lap record at the Nürburgring of no less than 71.83mph (115.6kph) – this was not beaten until 1952!

The most important event for BMW in 1939, however, was the Le Mans 24 Hours. A 328 coupé was built specially for this race with an aerodynamic body constructed by Touring of Milan on the *Superleggera* principle, with aluminium panels over a lightweight tubular framework. The engine was carefully blueprinted with much lighter reciprocating parts, stronger main bearings and a hotter camshaft. The carburettors, inlet tracts and valves were bigger. With higher than standard compression, output was around 120bhp at 5500rpm. The drivers of this 'Berlinetta', Prince Max zu Schaumburg-Lippe and Hans Wencher, won the 2-litre class at a record average of 82.5mph (132.8kph). There were also two standard 328 roadsters, driven by Roese/Heinemann and Brien/Scholz. Apart from dominating the 2-litre class, the 328s finished overall in fifth (the 'Berlinetta'), seventh and ninth (the roadsters)

places. They all proved capable of speeds approaching 125mph (200kph).

The second Mille Miglia for the 328s turned out to be rather different from the original. A car had gone off the road and killed several spectators in the 1938 race, so in consequence the Mille Miglia was not held in 1939, and the race staged in April 1940 – after the outbreak of war – was run over nine laps of a much shorter triangular course between Brescia, Cremona and Mantua. BMW brought five works cars to the start: the Le Mans 'Berlinetta' from 1939, three new roadsters with BMW's own aluminium-panelled bodywork, and a new BMW-built fastback coupé. With aerodynamic bodywork inspired by Professor Wunibald Kamm, this fastback coupé was built on the Touring principles and weighed only 1718lb (780kg), but drivers Count Giovanni Lurani and Franco Cortese had to retire with mechanical problems. The winner was the Le Mans 'Berlinetta' driven by Huschke von Hanstein and Walter Bäumer, who finished well ahead of the field at an average 103.6mph (166.7kph), with a fastest lap at more than 108mph (174kph). If the rest of the team had put up a better fight BMW might have scored à 1-2-3-4 victory; instead there was an Alfa Romeo in second place with the three 328 roadsters in close formation behind, in the order Adolf Brude/Ralph Roese, Wilhelm Briem/Ulrich Richter and Hans Wencher/Rudolf Scholz.

The 1940 Mille Miglia was won by Huschke von Hanstein and Walter Bäumer in the Touring-bodied aluminium coupé 328, which had already made its mark at Le Mans the year before.

All the Mille Miglia cars were fitted with tuned 120bhp engines and had top speeds of about 125mph (200kph), together with 0-62mph (100kph) acceleration of around 9sec. They had the standard cylinder block and head, however, and also the normal part-synchronised Hurth four-speed 'box with a final drive ratio of 3.44:1. The cars were equipped with the long-distance 22-gallon (100 litre) tanks and consumption of the special alcohol-petrol mixture was in the order of 15.3mpg (18.5 litres per 100km).

The original intention after the Mille Miglia was that the racers should take part in a race in Romania, so the three roadsters were driven under their own power to Brasov in the Carpathian mountains; but the race was cancelled and the three cars returned to Germany without having achieved anything. The subsequently twisted paths of the Mille Miglia cars can mostly be followed to this day. The Touring-built 'Berlinetta', now owned by an American enthusiast, appeared again at the 1993 Mille Miglia Storica, but BMW's own fastback coupé has completely disappeared. As mentioned earlier, H.J. Aldington brought one of the roadsters to Britain after the war, but in the 1970s this was bought back by BMW and is now found, completely restored, in the company's museum in Munich, and took part in the 1987 Mille Miglia Storica. One of the other two roadsters was once used by Hitler's armaments minister, Albert Speer, then 'liberated' by the Russians, and is now in a private collection in Riga in Latvia. The last of the roadsters went to the USA after the war and is still privately owned there.

The shape of these lightweight roadsters (less than 14cwt or 700kg) already pointed the way to the planned 328 replacement, scheduled to appear after the war when it was confidently expected to close the door on the competition from Alfa Romeo. In 1940-41, it appears that three more roadsters were built, again in co-operation with Touring, for the 1941 Berlin-Rome race, but this event was never held. These cars were to be fitted with a new six-cylinder engine with two overhead camshafts and some 140bhp, but this never happened and after the war these prototypes disappeared without trace. One survivor was subsequently discovered and is now in the Deutsches Museum in Munich.

The numerous victories of the 328 in Britain, Romania, Portugal, Argentina, Brazil, Africa, Switzerland

Period view of the Touring-bodied roadster built to take part in the 1941 Berlin-Rome race, which was cancelled – the car was never raced.

and above all Germany created the long-lived legend of this car. No other BMW has had such a beneficial influence on the image of the company as the 328, and the model has entered the record books as the most successful European sports car of the period.

The 328 on the road ....

The BMW 328 is more enjoyable to drive if you are somewhat shorter than my 6ft 1in! It is also preferable to have small feet (or at least avoid bulky footwear) and a long arm to reach the gear lever. But if you meet this description you are assured of a wonderful experience when you give one of the few surviving 328s its head.

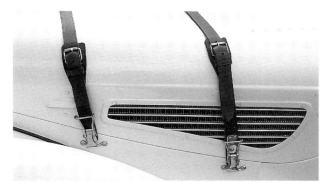

Characteristic ventilation louvres of the 328 bonnet: the leather straps are functional but also an important part of the look! Optional rear wheel spats made the 328 body more aerodynamic and improved top speed.

I drove the 1937 model from the BMW Museum, fitted with centre-lock wheels and spats over the rear wheels. This is used for a variety of events, including the Mille Miglia Storica, and is often driven by journalists or VIPs. Not least for this reason the original gearbox has been replaced with a Volvo all-synchro 'box (a ZF-based design that bolts straight onto a pre-war BMW), and the chassis has also been updated with additional anti-roll bars. Compared with a totally original 328, therefore, the gearchange is much simpler and easier, with no need for double-declutching. An earlier experience with a car fitted with the original gearbox was somewhat embarrassing for the first few miles, the gearbox protesting noisily at each attempted change. For a real expert who knows exactly how to match engine and road speeds, it would be different…

The 328, of course, is always driven with the soft-top down. There is a good reason for this: anyone over average height would find it very difficult to fit into the car with the soft-top up. The door sill is quite high, to the extent that it would be almost as easy to get into the car without bothering to open the doors. Hinged at the rear, they have handles only on the inside, with map pockets on the leather door trims. The large Bakelite – and almost vertical – steering wheel gets in the way dreadfully as you try to squeeze your legs into the car, but somehow you find the pedals, settle into the seat and pull the door shut.

The footwell is extremely narrow, with hardly any space between the accelerator and the brake pedal. The leather-upholstered seat squeezes you like a corset and can only be pushed back a couple of inches. Behind the seats is a tiny luggage space, mostly filled with the bits and pieces that somehow come together to support the soft-top. A camera bag and a couple of jackets fill the space available – creative packing is called for if you need to carry anything more. There is no access from the outside, where the shapely tail is dominated by the spare wheel and the petrol filler.

Straight ahead is the split windscreen, far too low for me and fitted with dinky little wipers; naturally the 'screen can be folded flat. Under the long bonnet sleep 80 willing horses, waiting for the call to life. The dashboard is simply tin, painted in the colour of the car. Right in front of the driver are two matching white dials the size of soup bowls, a speedometer reading to 180kph (over 110mph) and a tachometer that goes up to 5000rpm. In the traditional way both have their zeroes in the upper right-hand quadrant. Smaller dials indicate water temperature, oil pressure and fuel level. The

BMW's 'The ultimate driving machine' slogan could have been dreamed up for the 328 – a car that is truly a pleasure to drive, fast and hard.

Spartan, minimal and fast – the essence of a true sports car.

passenger has a small glovebox. There are controls for the radiator blind, lights and indicators, and other switches.

Turn the key, press the starter button and the six cylinders spring to life with a barely subdued roar. Careful pressure on the accelerator is gradually rewarded by the engine running more smoothly, and in a few seconds it seems to purr like a cat, as silkily as was promised in the old advertisements. The long cranked gear lever reaches up from the gearbox tunnel, crowned by a large Bakelite knob engraved with the normal H-pattern. The change is simple enough, but the aforementioned long arm is useful when you want first or third, in which case the lever disappears a long way forward under the dashboard...

Release the pistol-grip handbrake, let in the clutch, press on the loud pedal – and the car is off the leash, sprinting forward. The engine revs willingly, the car seems to eat the road. At over 4000rpm in second we are quickly doing 40mph, and the cockpit is filled with the glorious sound of the engine. Only the long movements of the gear lever are disappointing.

A 328 does not go round curves on the proverbial rails but turns out to have very much a will of its own. The rear end steps easily out of line and the car shows all the characteristics of an oversteerer. The indiscretions of the rear wheels, fortunately, are easily compensated for by the precision of the rack and pinion steering. You get used to the little ways of the 328, and after the first few

The interior is dominated by the almost vertical three-spoke steering wheel and the wonderful collection of instruments. The essentials are a 180kph speedometer and a rev counter reading to 5000rpm.

The small boot can only be reached from inside the car, so from the rear you only get at the spare wheel. The cockpit is fairly narrow, and tends to be cramped for a tall driver.

miles you lean instinctively into the curves as you would on a motorcycle. This is pure driving enjoyment!

What is really addictive is the impressive acceleration and the indescribable register of sound brought forth by the high-revving engine. It goes like a bomb, particularly in third, and seems able to run rings around anything else on the road. But the car has a mind of its own and gets the bit well between its teeth – any action from the driver seems to bring a reaction from the car. It is quite sensitive to side winds, requiring a firm grip on the wheel. Driving a 328 at 75mph is like driving a modern car at 125mph…

What about the brakes? Four drums and no servo mean that they need a determined push on the pedal. In a 328 you learn to look ahead and plan your driving – it is not a car to drive too forcefully. You are also aware of every single bump or pothole in the road, the narrow tyres and hard suspension transmitting plenty of information through the seat of your pants. It's not exactly a comfortable ride, but driving a 328 is like life: there's no gain without pain!

Exposed as you are on all sides to the rush of the wind, a ride in a 328 brings you near to nature – you can smell the grass and the flowers. The engine and the tyres perform a rare symphony, the car bucks under you like a race horse. Unlike modern cars which cocoon and isolate the driver, the 328 is all about communication. And the car runs so willingly, so utterly tirelessly.

Driving a 328 is an invigorating experience. It was not built just for getting from A to B, or even for promenading – it is a pure-blooded driving machine. Getting there is not just half the fun but *all* the fun. Is there any other pre-war car about which you could without hesitation say the same?

The BMW 328 is not a 'sensible' car. It is a challenge. It may be 60 years old but it is a timeless and beautiful high-performance car, guaranteed to inspire nostalgia. Like few other cars, the 328 is capable of winning your heart and mind alike…

BAVARIAN BAROQUE: 501–503

It took longer for BMW to start car production again after the war than most other German manufacturers. The main reason was that the pre-war car factory at Eisenach was now in the Soviet-occupied zone, later East Germany, and so beyond reach from Munich.

Actually, car production *did* start at Eisenach as early as October 1945. Later this became a problem and BMW had to go to court to get a ruling that the East German cars could not be called BMW. Henceforth the East German cars became EMW (for Eisenacher Motoren Werke), and for a time they sold quite well in some European export markets. Eisenach production included a barely-modified 327 cabriolet, and in 1951 EMW proposed a replacement for the 328 in the shape of its new 340S model – which must have caused consternation in Munich!

Embarking on production in Munich with a new model was extremely difficult because BMW literally had to start from scratch. The company's board persisted in

The 503 is supremely elegant, even with the electrically-powered soft-top raised.

Before anyone could even think of resuming car production in Munich after the war, this BMW/EMW 340S sports car was produced in Eisenach – but remained a one-off prototype.

This four-door convertible on the 502 chassis (right) was produced by BMW's 'tame' coachbuilder, Baur in Stuttgart. A full-width 500-series convertible (below) built by Swiss coachbuilder Ramseier of Worblaufen.

maintaining the policy that BMW must build exclusive luxury cars, even if the company was woefully short of production facilities: as BMW had no press shop of its own, the early post-war cars had bodies produced by the coachbuilder Baur in Stuttgart. For the new model, the 501, BMW stuck to the well-proven 2-litre overhead valve 'six', which nevertheless was persuaded to give 65bhp. The styling was claimed to be inspired by British ideas, with flowing wing lines like those found on contemporary Austins. Looking a little old-fashioned even when new, the unmistakable compound curves of these cars have inspired their German nickname of *Barockengel* – Baroque Angel.

At 1½ tons, the 501 was not exactly a lightweight sportster, yet it formed the basis for the first open BMWs built after the war. These had two- or four-door cabriolet bodies, constructed mainly by Baur, and appeared in 1954. In the same year, BMW produced a new alternative engine – the first series production aluminium V8 engine in the world. BMW's engineers had taken a look at developments in the USA and had decided that V8 engines were the coming thing, but they were well ahead of American car makers in using aluminium. On the other hand the single central camshaft was a traditional solution, adopted mainly for reasons of cost and simplicity.

The V8 originally was of 2.6 litres and developed 100bhp. It was fitted in the existing car, which now became the BMW 502 and weighed just 44lb (20kg) more than the six-cylinder model. A year later BMW introduced a 120bhp 3.2-litre V8, and with further development the bigger engine was eventually persuaded to produce 160bhp. Most of the convertibles were from now on fitted with the 3.2-litre engine.

Baur built around 200 two-door and 50 four-door cabriolets, with lined or unlined hoods – at the most a quarter of these had the six-cylinder engine. A 'six' can be distinguished from an 'eight' by the absence on the

With its small six-cylinder engine, the heavy 501 was chronically **underpowered – a lumbering dinosaur with dated looks.**

less powerful model of fog lamps and chrome trim strips. The Baur cabriolets were sold through the normal BMW dealer network and were comparatively affordable, costing exactly a third more than the standard saloons.

Other coachbuilders saw a business opportunity and began to build convertible or coupé versions of the Baroque Angels. The cars from Authenrieth in Darmstadt, which had built special bodies for BMWs before the war, were rather more expensive than the Baur versions at up to twice the price of a standard saloon, so only about 50 two-door and 10 four-door convertibles were turned out. The six different types of Authenrieth bodies were named after the German cities from where the first order for each was received, so they became the Bocholt, Koblenz, Darmstadt, Offenbach, Freiburg and Hannover types respectively. Some had completely different full-width bodies, quite unlike the BMW original.

Around half a dozen cars were fitted with individual bodies by other firms, such as Swiss coachbuilder Fritz Ramseier at Worblaufen near Bern, erstwhile pioneer of aerodynamic bodywork Wendler of Reutlingen, and boat builder Jacobsen & Steinberg of Berlin. Supposedly, the last-mentioned one-off body was partly designed by the eccentric stylist Luigi Colani and was only finished in the early 1960s. The body was made from glass-fibre and the car was fitted with the 160bhp 3.2-litre engine from what was by then called the BMW 3200 Super – Germany's fastest production saloon car.

The 502 was fitted with the more powerful V8 and some luxury touches **such as fog lamps; a 503 coupé is parked in the background.**

But all of these cars were big expensive barges, quite without any sporting pretensions. Then Max Hoffman brought BMW up sharply. Austrian-born Hoffman, who had become one of the leading importers of European cars in New York with interests ranging from Volkswagen to Jaguar, pointed out that the Baroque Angels were unsaleable in the US, that Mercedes-Benz had had a rousing success with the 300SL, and that BMW should get on with a replacement for the 328. Munich's response was to speed up development of two additional models. When one of the BMW designers left after a

The BMW 503 bore some family resemblance to the Baroque Angel saloons but was far more modern – as well as more elegant. This car (below) is a first series 503: the column gearchange is the clue.

The nose (right) is perhaps the least happy part of the 503's design – it seems implausible that the same designer created the racy 507! The tail-lamp clusters (below right) were similar on the 503 and the 507.

This attractive 3200 CS convertible was a one-off, built by Bertone in **Turin as a present for Herbert Quandt, BMW's majority shareholder.**

Jacobsen & Steinberg, a firm of boat builders in Berlin, built this one-off **502 convertible with a glass-fibre body; it has a certain 503 look.**

quarrel, BMW commissioned an idiosyncratic American freelance designer to complete their styling.

This was none other than the audacious Count Albrecht Goertz. Not only did he complete the styling of the new 507 roadster, but within only three months he designed a two-plus-two GT on a modified 502 chassis. There were both coupé and convertible versions of this new car, the 503, which made its debut at the Frankfurt International Motor Show in September 1955. The brand new cherry red convertible on the BMW stand impressed as one of the most elegant of the luxury performance cars of the time. Pinin Farina said that it was "the most beautiful car of the show". And yet the 503

would always be overshadowed by the even more striking 507, of which more anon…

For the 503, the 3.2-litre V8 engine was basically unchanged, but careful tuning and the use of two dual-choke downdraught carburettors took power up to 140bhp at 4800rpm, enough for a top speed of 118mph (190kph). Even if the 503 was not quite a sports car, it certainly had sufficient power. The chassis, running on big 16in wheels, was taken over from the 502 with little change. The front track was almost 3in (70mm) wider, but suspension was similar, with longitudinal torsion bars front and rear, independent only at the front. The gearbox was originally mounted separately, as on the 501/502 saloons, on the chassis crossmember below the front seat, and a column change was used. On the second series 503 in 1957, however, the gearbox was in unit with the engine and the chassis modified accordingly, and these later cars had a floor change – and some were also fitted with front disc brakes.

The 503 was a substantial car at a substantial price. Coupé and convertible models cost the same, DM 29,500, which was DM 7000 less than a Mercedes-Benz 300S convertible or coupé. The second series cars of 1957 were introduced at DM 31,500, and by the end of 1958 the price had crept up to DM 32,950. In Britain, where the price was inflated by import duty and purchase tax, the 503 cost an astronomical £4801 in October 1957, almost as much, staggeringly, as a Bentley S-type saloon at £5544.

The main reason for the high price was that the 503 was always built by hand. From May 1956 to May 1960, only 409 examples were built, of which a mere 138 were

convertibles. Most of the body panels were of aluminium but some of the early cars had steel doors. By contemporary standards equipment was lavish, with electric windows, full heating and ventilation, laminated windscreen, 16½-gallon (75-litre) tank, luggage compartment lamp, and – on the convertible – an electrically-operated soft-top. An automatic gearbox was never offered.

In the British gangster movie *The Last Run*, made in 1971, a brown 503 convertible featured, fitted with overdrive. This was never a factory offering and seems to have been a special modification for George C. Scott. How tragic that this fine car – there may even have been two used for the film – was crushed so brutally!

The 501, 502 and 503 convertibles would be the last big BMW soft-top cars for many a year. The 503 replacement, the Bertone-designed 3200 CS, was not offered in convertible form – even if BMW's majority shareholder Herbert Quandt had such a car built as a one-off for his personal use in 1963. A new BMW six-

A 503 cabriolet had a role in the film *The Last Run*, made in 1971 and starring George C. Scott.

cylinder convertible only appeared in 1977 and then this model again had a Baur body. An eight-cylinder convertible was only on the cards for the second half of the 1990s…

The Baroque Angels and their derivatives were spectacular cars – and also lost a spectacular amount of money for BMW. It has been estimated that each of the 500-series cars was sold at a loss of some DM 5000. At the end of production these expensive limousines were ruthlessly discounted, probably because by 1963 BMW had need of its production facilities for more profitable products. The 500-series cars might have ruined BMW completely, and the company was really only saved by the Isetta 'bubble' car and the 700-series two-cylinder small car, which bridged the gap until the long-awaited first 'real BMW' of the post-war period appeared in 1963 – the first of the 'new class', the 1500 saloon.

DESIGN CLASSIC: 507

L ove blinds you. How else can we explain that the hard-boiled businessmen in charge of almost-bankrupt BMW decided to go ahead with a sports car that could never bring any profit? Had they taken leave of their senses? All they had seen before their decision was a selection of sketches and a fifth-scale model, prepared by a gentleman amateur and *bon vivant* who had long since departed for the USA. The story of this car is like a flight of fantasy, with enough human suffering to fill a Greek tragedy.

It all began with Max Hoffman in the USA. He spun a convincing tale and made some wild promises. He promised BMW that if it built a really attractive sports car, he could easily sell at least 1000 in the US market. The 50-year-old Austro-American was not simply a con man: he had done good business with the successful Mercedes-Benz 190SL and 300SL, and had prompted Porsche to build the Speedster version of the 356A.

An original brochure illustration, showing a stylised 507 with whitewall tyres in a suitably modern, glamorous setting.

Meanwhile, the former BMW racing team manager, Ernst Loof, whose Veritas company at the Nürburgring was struggling to survive, heard about Hoffman's ideas in 1954. Loof saw his opportunity and struck like lightning: he went to see BMW's chairman, Kurt Donath, ill in hospital. Loof was not a welcome visitor at the sick-bed, and to get rid of him Donath is finally supposed to have said, "All right, go ahead and build your car – but use the V8 engine, it's ready now".

Loof was a tragic figure, a dreamer, who had had a lot of bad luck with his Veritas projects; now he had to be satisfied with the occasional crumb thrown to him from the BMW table. At that time aged 54, Loof took a 502 chassis, shortened the wheelbase by 14in (35cm), added a

BMW celebrated the 40th anniversary of the 507 in September 1995. Guests of honour were Count Albrecht Goertz, the designer, and John Surtees, long-time 507 owner who in the 1950s evaluated disc brake installation for BMW. Held at BMW's design centre in Munich, the event saw an impressive cavalcade of 507s and a great party trick!

few ideas of his own such as a five-speed ZF gearbox and some improvements inspired by his racing experience. He built the wooden formers for the bodywork which was then executed in aluminium by Baur of Stuttgart. The resulting two-seater looked just like a twin of Loof's earlier Veritas Nürburg RS2, and somewhat like a bloated caricature of an MGA…

To BMW this became the 507a. The prototype was given the chassis number 70,001, a magic number as the first in what became the number sequence for all later 507s. The Loof car figured in the BMW main catalogue in the autumn of 1954 as the '502 sports model'. Hoffman, however, would have none of it, bluntly declaring that he could not sell this dreadful-looking thing in America, and that if BMW were so incompetent he would find an Italian designer to do the job properly.

Most unfortunately, Loof decided to do his own thing with 'his' new prototype. He took it to the concours d'élégance at Bad Neuenahr in September 1954 where the car promptly won an award – but also received a lot of bad publicity. Not only did most journalists find the car ugly, but to a man they felt cheated because the car had not been shown to the press before it simply appeared at a public event. BMW's sales director Grewenig forbade any further public appearances of the car, and Loof was so sickened that the episode may have contributed to his early death in 1956.

Everything was up in the air again. The temperamental Hoffman, a former racing driver who was forever bemoaning the passing of the 328, could not

come up with the promised Italian designer – but found a local alternative. Right there in New York was a German nobleman who had trained with industrial designer Raymond Loewy and now ran his own small studio, which he described as "just a rather good one-man show". This was the 40-year-old Count Albrecht Goertz, who had never before designed a car. Given the nod by Hoffman, he sent a few sketches to Munich, even daring to commit sacrilege by converting the double kidneys of the BMW grille to a pair of slim, horizontal, oval nostrils. He also proposed extra grilles on the front wings. Obviously influenced by American as well as Italian styling, his ideas impressed the managers at Munich and they wanted to know more of the Count and his work.

It was Goertz's view that the 300SL was 'too masculine': the Americans wanted softer, more feminine shapes, and this was just what he could deliver. Although quite without experience in the field of automotive

design, he was soon discussing his ideas with BMW's new chief designer, Wilhelm Hofmeister. The result was that Goertz was taken on as a consultant, with an annual fee of DM 80,000. From December 1954 he shuttled between New York and Munich to oversee the full-scale clay model taking shape, with rising young designer Johann König in charge of the work. The basis for the car was the short-wheelbase chassis proposed by Loof, but all further engineering development was the responsibility of 56-year-old Fritz Fiedler, who by now had returned to his position as BMW's chief engineer. Fiedler did his utmost to accommodate the most fanciful of Goertz's ideas and was rewarded by the Count with the nickname 'Mr No Problem'. Night after night Fiedler stood bent over his drawing board to get the car ready in time for launch at the Frankfurt International Motor Show in September 1955.

Baron Alexander von Falkenhausen, BMW's racing manager, was responsible for the detailed design of the chassis and brakes, liaising closely with Fiedler and project leader Alfred Böning – an early and very successful example of teamwork. Naturally the engine was to be the 3.2-litre V8, and equally natural was the choice of two double-choke carburettors to improve output. High-compression pistons were also used, although the standard camshaft and valve timing were retained. The engine gave some 140bhp on the test bed. Any particularly powerful engine was picked out for the new roadster – engines slightly below par were put to one side for use in the 503 models. So although the 507 engine was not very scientifically tuned or modified, BMW soon began to claim 150bhp at 5000rpm.

This 507 forerunner (top) was the work of Ernst Loof and resembles his Veritas cars. An alternative fifth-scale design (above) had a sharper look and pronounced tail fins.

Rather more development was put into the chassis, as the possibility of using the 507 in motor sport was taken into consideration from the start. Of course the body was to be made of aluminium – as was appropriate for a sports car – but the solid chassis meant that the 507 was not exactly a lightweight, at over 25cwt (1280kg).

Goertz's favourite way of admiring his creation was from above. He would perch at the top of a step-ladder and describe it in fulsome prose: "Timeless elegance – clean, sweeping lines – gentle curves and soft creases. The wheels must be prominent, they are the most beautiful part of a car. A sports car must resemble a race horse – it must express movement even when it stands still." Certainly the Count placed the wheels so far outside the bodywork that they not only became an aesthetic feature but also threw up a lot of dirt...

When Hoffman saw the design he rashly promised that he could sell 2000 or even 3000, as long as the price

Designer Johann König put plenty of effort – and plenty of clay – into the full-scale 507 model (top). Count Goertz, pictured with his final fifth-scale model (which later graced the desk of a senior BMW executive), paid regular visits from the USA to check on progress.

Even the interior, seen here on the show prototype, was all new and unique, the only carry-over component from the saloons being the chrome-plated ashtray.

was no more than $5000, then DM 20,000. Slowly but surely, three running prototypes were completed, initially with excessively thin aluminium panelling. The actual 1955 motor show car was completed without engine or brakes. Nobody noticed the omission – except for the hapless mechanic who had to transport the car back to Munich after the show debut. Letting the car roll down a ramp, he discovered too late the absence of brakes and ran it smack into a wall. But by then the bright white car had already become the star of the 1955 Frankfurt show, outshining the other new BMW models, the 503 GT and the 505 limousine.

The 1955 show car was a hand-built prototype, fitted with a hard-top for publicity photographs.

The bonnet of the 507 hides this 3.2-litre version of the BMW push-rod overhead valve V8 engine.

More important was the unveiling in New York that had occurred two months earlier, in the Waldorf Astoria Hotel. The tight-fitting, curvy bodywork aroused the desires even of the prim Americans. The popular press described the car as a 'sex bomb on wheels' and claimed that Goertz had drawn inspiration from Sophia Loren or Gina Lollobrigida. Despite all the publicity, not many orders were taken – at the US presentation BMW put the price at around $9000 (DM 36,000). Hoffman withdrew his optimistic forecasts: the price was too high and the car was not competitive against the popular Chevrolet Corvette and Ford Thunderbird, which both cost less than $4000.

This was perhaps the point where BMW should have pulled the plug on the project. While the 507's price in Germany was fixed at DM 26,000, this was simply to

The original prototype, chassis number 70,002, as it is today. The filler cap on first series models is above the right-hand rear wing.

The 24-gallon tank is directly behind the seats on a first series car, with a lockable compartment above the tank.

Ventilation louvres in the front wings dominate the side view – and have echoes of contemporary Ferrari and Mercedes-Benz sports cars.

Front and rear views are both well designed – testimony to Goertz's brilliant eye.

keep it below the DM 29,000 that a 300SL Gullwing coupé cost. In the USA, for a time the 507 cost $1000 more than the Mercedes! In Britain, import duty and purchase tax drove the price of a 507 up to an impossible £4201 in October 1957, more than twice an XK150. Still, the 507 had the eternal rivals at Stuttgart so worried that they quickly began to develop an alternative 300SL Roadster, sharing its 3-litre six-cylinder engine with the Gullwing coupé. Mercedes–Benz sold seven times more 300SL Roadsters than BMW sold 507s…

The rumour of the new Mercedes put the wind up BMW, which postponed series production of the 507 to spare its customers any teething troubles resulting from inadequate development. It was a full 14 months after the Frankfurt debut when the first 507s went out to customers. BMW also took its time building each car:

The dashboard of a first series 507, with the characteristic deep scuttle panel. This car was experimentally fitted with a VDO rev counter reading to 7000rpm.

One of the most famous 507 owners was Elvis Presley, who bought his car while on service with the American forces in Germany.

after final assembly each 507 was passed to the experimental department for a 100km road test and only then despatched to sales.

Most customers ordered the 507 roadster complete with aluminium hard-top. This fits so well that hard-top cars are often assumed to be fixed-head coupés. With the hard-top in place, the drag coefficient of a 507 was an average 0.442, but for those who wanted to improve the aerodynamics a complete aluminium undershield was available. A tonneau cover was also available for the car, and at least one 507 was fitted with a special racing windscreen. The most common type of wheel was the centre-lock disc, as cast alloy wheels were not yet available. The preferred colour scheme for the 507 was white with red leather upholstery, but there was a choice of 30 different colours, including more discreet shades such as grey or beige.

The 507 sales brochure claimed a top speed of 220kph, almost 137mph. Not everybody believed this, so, following the Mercedes-Benz example, BMW staged a demonstration run on a closed section of *Autobahn*. A specially prepared 507 fitted with a higher rear axle ratio, hard racing tyres and aerodynamic aids reached a true speed of 223kph (138.5mph) – but most normal production cars reached only around 200kph (125mph). Acceleration was excellent, 0–100kph (62mph) taking 11.1sec, which was as quick as a Porsche 356 Carrera; in

28.2sec the car reached 160kph (99.4mph). The unique feature of the 507 was the flexibility of its engine, with bags of torque from 1500 to 5000rpm – here, at least, the 300SL was beaten.

The first series of 507s, built until June 1957, could be recognised by the large 110-litre (24-gallon) tank directly behind the seats, and by the dashboard with the top rail pulled down low. At the end of the first series the contract with designer Goertz, much to his puzzlement, was allowed to expire, and he would only work again for BMW some ten years later. In between he worked for Nissan, where he was godfather to the 240Z, and then for Porsche, where he submitted proposals for the 356

The Loewy-bodied 507, based on a first series chassis, may be seen today in the Petersen Museum in Los Angeles.

replacement and for a 914/6 prototype. In the following years he designed anything from fountain pens to saucepans, from cameras to sports clothes – and always had new ideas. He never owned a 507, but has an enthusiastic fan club of 507 owners.

The second series of the 507 reached higher production figures. The design was somewhat simplified but the price was increased to DM 28,500. There was a new dashboard, a much deeper design in which there was also room for the radio loudspeaker, but the instrumentation was unchanged, still with two large dials in front of the driver – tachometer to 6000rpm, speedometer to 250kph or 160mph – and a small clock

positioned between them. A parcel shelf behind the seats was a great improvement, while the seats themselves could be adjusted further rearwards thanks to a smaller 65-litre (14-gallon) tank under the boot floor, with the filler cap now on the right-hand side at the back. However, the separate lockable compartment previously found above the petrol tank had sadly disappeared.

Such comforts as an automatic gearbox, a powered soft-top and power steering were never available. However, at least the position of the four-spoke steering wheel could be adjusted, unlike on the 503. For customers in hot climates, a tropical radiator was available. But buyers in Britain, Sweden, Australia and

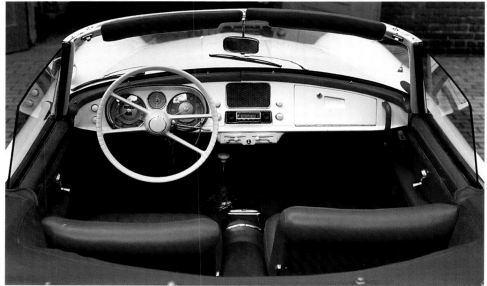

The thinly-lined soft-top is not just for dire need and complements the lines of the car. On the second series 507 (left) the actual dash panel was deeper, allowing room for the radio loudspeaker.

Press, grip and pull: the door handle of the 507 is a talking point.

Japan had to put up with left-hand drive – the 507 was never available with right-hand drive. Nor was it ever offered with a more powerful engine, or with disc brakes. The last in particular was an omission, as in 1959 BMW brought out the 3.2-litre Super as the first German production car with disc brakes. Hard-driving VIP customers such as John Surtees had their cars specially modified by BMW, Surtees himself playing a significant development role in having all-round Dunlop discs fitted to the 507 that he bought new and still owns today.

Among famous 507 owners were Elvis Presley, film stars Alain Delon and Ursula Andress, opera singer Mario del Monaco, world-class skier Toni Sailer, Prince Rainier of Monaco and the Aga Khan – mostly people for whom style was more important than speed. BMW 507s also appeared in a number of movies – but James Bond never drove one. Although sporty and beautiful, the 507 was never really the sort of car that one drove to the full extent of its performance – more cruiser than bruiser.

With BMW's financial position getting steadily

The most characteristic feature of the 507's nose are the two oval grilles – a distant relative of BMW's twin kidneys.

Michelotti's one-off 507 was a functional roadster with hard-top. While BMW showed no interest in this car, it did use a Michelotti design for the 700.

worse, there was less and less reason for the 507's existence, and production came to an end in December 1959. Only two 507s were fitted with special bodywork: one was a futuristic coupé by Raymond Loewy, the other a Michelotti convertible with hard-top, quite functional but with embryonic tail fins.

Goertz made several proposals for a modernised 507, or a high-performance replica of his favourite design. Rumour also has it that BMW chairman Bernd Pischetsrieder and engineering chief Wolfgang Reitzle

are intrigued by the idea of a modern 507 to give BMW an open car in the prestige category. Inside information from Munich suggests that there may be a project E52, a modern interpretation of the 507, which could see limited production before the year 2000.

The 507 in motor sport ....

Although the 507 looks as if it were built for racing, its creators had no intention of going in for either GT or

touring car events, for the simple reason that homologation required a minimum production of 100 cars for the GT class or 1000 for the touring car category – and the 507 only reached the lower figure at the end of 1957. Besides, it would not have been competitive against more specialised and powerful GT racers from companies such as Ferrari, Maserati and Porsche.

BMW's racing manager, von Falkenhausen, realised that there were only limited possibilities with the stock pushrod V8 engine, but nevertheless had a team of three works racers built. With hotter camshafts and bigger carburettors, the engines gave some 190bhp. The racers were also fitted with five-speed gearboxes, limited slip differentials and disc brakes. They invariably ran with hard-tops.

The most famous of the 507 works drivers was Hans Stuck, who had scored a number of victories in the pre-war Auto Union Grand Prix racers. Now in his 50s, he was the sales manager for the sporting BMWs, and his appearances in the 507 were mainly for publicity – but he still managed to beat the Ferraris and 300SLs, notably in

Two victories for Hans Stuck in 1959: in the ADAC hillclimb at Schauinsland near **Freiburg (top), and in the Austrian Mountain Grand Prix at the Gaisberg hillclimb (above).**

hillclimbs. In 1958 he was GT category winner in the over 2-litre or over 2.6-litre classes in the Rossfeld hillclimb, the Schauinsland hillclimb and the Swiss Mountain Grand Prix – all of which counted towards the

Normally the 507 is a dogged understeerer – only when cornering very quickly does the tail begin to step out.

European Hillclimb Championship. The following year Stuck could count victories in the Wallberg race, again in the Rossfeld and Schauinsland hillclimbs and the Swiss mountain race, in races at Gaisberg and Wurzenpass, and even in the Austrian GP at the Salzburgring, where he put up a race average of 88kph (55mph).

Few other laurels were gathered by the 507. BMW's race manager, von Falkenhausen, won the GT class of the 1957 Adria rally, and BMW dealer Helm Glöckler was placed third in the 1958 Schauinsland race. Swiss driver Robert Jenny won the GT class in the 'imitation' Mille Miglia at Brescia in 1958. Finally Arthur Heuberger won the GT classes in the Kandersty hillclimb, the Innsbruck airport race and the Geneva rally, all in 1958.

The 507 on the road ....

Unlike the cramped and uncomfortable 328, the 507 will easily accommodate drivers of above-average stature – at least in the case of the second series cars where the seats can be adjusted further back. One small peculiarity – shared with some contemporary Italian sports cars such as the Fiat 8V – is that you must first press a button to release the counter-sunk door handle. A little care is needed as you get into the car: the petrol tap is immediately inside the door sill, and if this has been turned to the reserve position it is likely to catch your trouser leg. However, this is a useful reminder that you need to fill the tank…

The leather seats are wide but offer little side support – sporting drivers often prefer to replace them with bucket seats. The pedals are well positioned as you sit up close to the almost vertical steering wheel. The pistol-grip handbrake hides below the steering wheel on the left. The short gear lever is far forward on the centre tunnel, almost under the dashboard. The dash panel is painted in the body colour and has a simple, timeless design, with large VDO dials and – on the car I tried – a splendid Blaupunkt self-seeking radio with automatic aerial. There are map pockets in the leather door trims but these are only accessible when the door is open…

Starting up, the engine comes alive with a soft burbling noise, a sound far more quiet and refined that the seductive roar of a Ferrari or Jaguar. The clutch is rather heavy, but otherwise the controls are easy to operate. The gearchange requires no muscle power at all and is beautifully precise, but it is a pity that there are only four speeds – five-speed boxes were reserved for the works racers. However, smart owners have discovered that a five-speed version of the ZF gearbox used in the 1960s Maseratis will fit easily in a 507. Driving a converted five-speed 507 on another occasion clearly demonstrated that the extra ratio makes the car even better to drive.

Whatever the gearbox, there is no doubt that the 507 has impressive performance. Exploring the higher reaches of revs, the engine sound changes to the more sporting note that you would expect from a car with the looks of the 507. In one test, 82 decibels were measured – you almost wish it was more! Pushing towards top speed, you

approach the red zone on the tachometer at 5700rpm, which corresponds to 112mph (180kph) in fourth gear. The faster you go, the more fun the car is to drive, the more agile it seems to be. The 507 is so easy to control that you hardly realise how quickly it goes.

The big 16in wheels were originally fitted with Continental cross-ply tyres which lost their grip beyond the 100mph mark, but nowadays most cars run on wider Pirelli 185 radials which will foul the wheelarches unless the body is raised on extra spacers. Long, sweeping curves are the speciality of the 507, the car reacting precisely to the smallest movement of the steering wheel, even at high speeds. The car will only oversteer if you power through a sharp curve too quickly – but even so you are given plenty of advance warning. In normal driving, the 507 is an obstinate understeerer which hardly gives any opportunity to explore the thrills of driving on the edge. When you want to stop, the servo-assisted drum brakes prove to be utterly safe and stop the car in a straight line – braking performance is better than, for

example, contemporary Aston Martins. This is 'active safety', BMW-style.

Although no racer, the 507 is certainly a touring sports car, but one with a dual personality – it is just as happy to cruise the boulevards or promenade through the city. The engine is so torquey, so relaxed and untemperamental that you only need to change down if the revs drop below 1000rpm. Whatever the speed, the ride is comfortable. Even at high speeds with the soft-top down you do not get blown out of the car – and with the side windows wound up the cockpit remains calm.

The 507 is wonderful to drive. This car really should have a poetic name – something like *Emotio* or *Bella* or *Simpatico*. You would not call it nimble and it only becomes a real sprinter when you apply the spurs – but the car is too civilised to be treated brutally.

OPEN SEASON: COMPACT CABRIOS FROM '02' TO M3

A fter its brush with bankruptcy, BMW began its return to financial health with the small 700 model, fitted with a bored-out flat-twin motorcycle engine in the rear, and with up to 40bhp in its most powerful versions. Between 1961-64 a convertible model was part of the 700 range, but this was to be the last drophead BMW for some years, and there were no further thoughts of luxury convertibles. Instead, BMW concentrated on saloon cars, the 'new class' series starting with the 1500 in 1963, and leading on to the 1600, 1800 and 2000 models that finally pulled the BMW balance sheet firmly back into the black.

The 'new class' was ultimately replaced by the first 5-series, but meanwhile BMW brought out the compact '02' range, starting with the 1600-2 (later simply the 1602) in 1966. Known internally as Project 114, the '02' range resembled the four-door 2000 but was almost 11in (27cm) shorter and rather prettier. The '02' designation indicated two doors – there was at that time no intention of making a small four-door model. As the '02' range

The Baur-bodied 1600-2 was a full convertible, and some 2002s also had this type of body. Smallest **ever drophead from BMW was the rear-engined 700 (below), with styling by Michelotti.**

developed, the ultimate version was the 2002 Turbo of 1973. These compact sports saloons were everything that die-hard BMW enthusiasts could wish for, and it is not surprising that a 1602 cabriolet model soon appeared.

The full convertible of the 2002 was replaced by this 'safety convertible' with a roll-over bar, which also made the body much more rigid.

The first such car appeared at the Frankfurt Motor Show in 1967, fitted with a standard 85bhp 1.6-litre engine. It was particularly admired for its soft-top, which folded away completely out of sight.

This two-plus-two convertible was developed and built by Baur in Stuttgart. However, with the roof completely chopped off, the car was insufficiently rigid and also prone to rust. Nevertheless from late 1967 to late 1971 Baur built precisely 1682 examples of the 1602 convertible, each of which cost DM 11,980 – DM 3000 more than the standard saloon. In 1971 there were also 256 examples of a similarly-bodied 2002 convertible, fitted with the 100bhp 2-litre engine. But then that was it for the time being: for the next 14 years BMW did not offer a fully convertible car!

Instead BMW took a leaf out of the Porsche book, imitating the Targa concept of the 911 and 914 models. The result was the 2002 targa convertible introduced in 1971. With a fully integrated roll-over bar and fixed roof rails, it was far more rigid than its predecessor. The front roof panel was rigid and stowed away in the boot, while the rear soft-top was of fabric and folded down in the normal way. This car was also a joint project with Baur, which undertook final assembly from parts supplied by BMW. The resulting car cost DM 14,985 and remained

in production until June 1975, the total run being 2272 cars. Baur was to remain true to this concept for many years after, building more than 15,000 similar cars up to the mid-1980s.

In mid-1975 the '02' was replaced by the first 3-series (project E21). The new body was simpler and more functional, but the car was somewhat bigger and more expensive. The typically wide range embraced the following models with different engine sizes: 315, 316, 318 and 320 with carburettor four-cylinder engines; from 1977 a new six-cylinder 320; and the fuel-injected 318i, 320i and 323i. From 1977 to 1983, Baur built targa versions, officially called 'hard top cabriolets', of all of these 3-series models. Around 4600 of these cars were made, typically costing DM 7500 more than the equivalent saloons. Karmann, the Osnabrück coachbuilder which supplied BMW with coupé bodywork, also built a prototype 3-series convertible but this did not go into production.

The second 3-series (project E30) appeared in 1983, still originally only with two-door coachwork, but now every model in the range, apart from the bargain-basement 1.6-litre car, had fuel-injected engines. Baur again offered a targa model according to its traditional recipe, and most of the Baur cars were based on the 320i

The first 3-series (type E21) was not available as a full convertible, only with this targa-type Baur body (right), but was sold through the normal BMW network. After the appearance of the second 3-series (type E30) Baur continued to offer its own targa version (below).

with the 125bhp 2-litre 'six'. The Baur conversions, in Germany at least, had one particular advantage: they were classified as 'saloons' by the insurance companies and so attracted lower premiums than proper convertibles. But they did not appeal to all fresh air enthusiasts – the targa style was not the same as a fully opening convertible.

BMW scored a bull's eye when it launched its own two-plus-two convertible with a fully disappearing hood at the 1985 Frankfurt Motor Show, this model going into series production in BMW's new factory at Regensburg in May 1986. The car was a remarkable success: the most popular model in the range was the 171bhp 325i of which 79,000 were built, but there were also 33,000 320i convertibles (129bhp) and almost 23,000 318i convertibles (113bhp). Prices ranged from DM 43,000 to DM 54,000, and the list of options was typically lengthy, one extra being a lightweight hard-top weighing only 60lb (27kg). From September 1987 catalysts were fitted for the German home market, while a powered soft-top became optional in 1990.

Baur still persisted with the targa-type cabriolet, which was offered until 1991 on the 316i, 318i, 320i and 325i (or iX) models. Some 15,000 were made, at prices ranging from DM 35,000 to DM 60,000. In addition, there were to be two extraordinary derivatives of the

most potent 325i model: one was BMW's own Z1 roadster, developed by the subsidiary company BMW-Technik, while the other was the Wiesmann roadster, offered by a North German coachbuilder. Both are described in detail in the next chapter.

By far the fastest version of the 3-series convertible was the M3 model. This was fitted with the M30 engine, a 2.3-litre 16-valve twin cam 'four' that had been developed from the engine of the M1 sports racing car, built by BMW Motorsport. In the M3 this engine originally gave 200bhp, later improved to 215bhp. These cars also had lowered suspension, wider track and wheels, and aerodynamic improvements. The result was a top speed of almost 150mph (240kph) and 0-62mph (100kph) acceleration in only 7.3sec. A prototype was shown at Frankfurt in 1987 and the response was so positive that the car soon went into production. The 200bhp M3 convertible was made from May 1988 to June 1991, with 786 of these cars finding buyers. Each paid more than DM 90,000 for the privilege of owning the most powerful open BMW yet and enjoying the sound of a barely tamed racing car. The 215bhp version remained in production until 1993.

Although most of the 3-series cars were replaced by the third incarnation of this model (the E36 range) in 1990, the E30 type convertibles stayed in production until 1993, when they were replaced by new models based on the coupé version of the E36. At the time of writing there are three versions of this convertible: the eight-valve 318i with 115bhp, the 16-valve 320i with 150bhp, and the six-cylinder 24-valve 328i with 193bhp. As a one-off experiment, BMW Motorsport built a 325tds convertible with the 143bhp turbo diesel engine but this was not put into production – the additional tax on diesel-engined cars in Germany means that there is no market for diesel convertibles.

When BMW introduced its own full convertible of the 3-series, customer demand exceeded every expectation.

M3 Cabrio

The first M3, still with a four-cylinder engine, was also available in convertible form (above); this version went into production in May 1988.

Even more attractive was the coupé-based convertible version of the third 3-series (type E36), introduced in 1993.

The M3 version (above) features a 3.2-litre six-cylinder engine and carefully developed running gear.

The present four-door targa convertible from Baur is a clever idea. Independently of each other, the top panels can be removed or the rear soft-top folded.

Of course, these 3-series convertibles are not that sporting, and far removed from the spartan roadster ideal – which BMW would eventually return to with other models. With the 3-series the emphasis is on refinement, luxury and a high level of standard equipment; the main options are an automatic gearbox, a hard-top and a powered soft-top. The latter is not really required, not even for the women customers who form a large proportion of convertible buyers. BMW has developed manual soft-tops which are state-of-the-art when it comes to ease of operation. Exhaustive tests have been carried out to ensure that long fingernails remain unbroken by BMW soft-tops!

The icing on the cake in the new range is the M3 convertible, introduced at the end of 1993 with a 294bhp 3-litre six-cylinder engine – and two years later fitted with the even more powerful 321bhp 3.2-litre engine. Fitted with a six-speed gearbox and a limited slip differential as standard, this is almost the ultimate BMW convertible. It is a worthy rival even for the Porsche 911, and even at DM 97,500 it works out cheaper than the Zuffenhausen classic. The new M3 achieves 0-62mph (100kph) in 5.6sec and the top speed is limited electronically to 155mph (250kph) – without the speed limiter the car could probably reach 175mph. From the outside, the extra power of the M3 version is only apparent from the lowered suspension, wider tyres and the oil cooler. Similarly impressive performance is offered by the Alpina B3 convertible, which is available from selected BMW dealers.

For the future, there are rumours about a convertible version of the new 1996 5-series with the lightweight aluminium suspension. Whether such a version ever goes into production probably depends on what the European competitors get up to. BMW keeps a close eye on new projects from Mercedes-Benz in particular, but also from Audi and Jaguar.

Many small coachbuilders have specialised for a long time in after-market conversions of BMWs. This kind of work does not come cheap: Lumma of Winterlingen or Peters of Delbrück will relieve you of DM 15,000 to convert your two-door '02' or early 3-series into a full convertible. Meanwhile, BMW's long-standing 'tame' coachbuilder, Baur, continues undeterred to produce the targa-type cabriolets, but after the introduction of the E36-type 3-series these are now built exclusively on the basis of the *four*-door saloon.

With this version it seems that Baur has found a niche all of its own: the Baur TC four-door is a unique proposition in today's market, appealing strongly to the non-conformist. These cars preserve the roominess and comfort of the standard five-seater, yet offer greater driving pleasure with the combination of a removable targa roof and a folding rear hood. With their multi-opening roofs, these cars are reminiscent of the classic landaulet type of body. You can buy one from DM 52,000 and upwards, Baur offer all the various models – 316i, 318i, 320i and 328i – and in 1995 even introduced the diesel models, 318tds and 325tds, at DM 55,000 and DM 64,000 respectively. From November 1992 to the end of 1995, production of these four-door cabriolets totalled some 300 cars.

PLASTIC SCULPTURE: Z1

"Really, the whole point of the Z1 is the door." So joked an engineer from BMW-Technik as he pushed the button to operate the electric door lift of the spectacular plastic roadster. Founded in 1985, BMW-Technik has become the company's own think tank. Working a stone's throw from the 'four-cylinder' skyscraper that is BMW's headquarters in Munich, around 100 specialists develop new designs and technologies for the company's future. It took them three years to develop the unique Z1 – which in turn became the trendsetter for the modern sports car renaissance.

Responsible for the project were chief engineer Dr Ulrich Bez and designer Harm Lagaay. Bez admits that they did not concern themselves greatly with the feasibility of actually manufacturing the car. To reach a profitable production level – estimated as 30,000 cars annually – the Z1 would have required its own all-new production facility. Bez, who has since created an entire new model range for the Korean car manufacturer Daewoo, worked at BMW between 1982-88. As well as

The Z1 is a car that arouses curiousity, for its striking overall shape as well as its slide-down doors. The Z1 interior (opposite top) borrowed heavily from the ordinary 3-series. Under the bonnet (right) is the 170bhp single overhead cam six-cylinder engine from the 325i version of the E30 range. The easily stripped plastic skin (below) that is fixed to the car's solid hull – body repairs should be simple!

The original Z1 prototype: narrower air intakes in the bumper and slightly different headlamp fairings distinguish it.

being the begetter of the Z1, for his former employer Porsche he created the futuristic 'Panamericana' which anticipated the shape of the current 911 Targa. He even went so far as to sketch a Z3-like roadster intended as a shared BMW-Porsche project, with different bodies on the same platform.

The first Z1 study had been shown by BMW to the press in August 1986, touted as the first product of the Technik subsidiary. At this time, there was one styling mock-up and one running prototype. The project brief had called for a car which represented 'freedom on four wheels' and which was 'young, dynamic and cheeky'. With undershield, spoilers and aerodynamic aids it was to be a ground-effect car, with negative lift front and rear. Another aim was to create a car which could be driven in open form without cockpit turbulence. The compact car was described as having 'almost square' proportions. A particular feature was the 'front-centre' engine – not a good solution from a packaging point of view but offering the ideal 50/50 front/rear weight distribution. Four-wheel drive, at that time still unusual enough to be thought of as futuristic, was also considered.

Sceptics in the press wondered whether BMW could be serious. They were only convinced when the Z1 production car appeared at the 1987 Frankfurt Motor Show. The design created a sensation, with unique features such as its vertically sliding doors and the then still unusual high-intensity headlamps. Here was a car which combined progressive, forward-looking technology with all the appeal of a classic roadster. The galvanised chassis was bonded together with a plastic floorpan, and all skin panels were made from recyclable plastic material. The shape was strictly functional and 'cool' – it was not intended to be a car you were emotional about.

In terms of its engineering, the Z1 was closely based on the contemporary 325i, with a six-cylinder 12-valve engine, but the structure was very different. At 96.5in (2.45m), the Z1 wheelbase was some 5in (12cm) shorter than the 3-series, the overall length of 157.5in (4m) being unusually compact. For comparison, the 1986 prototype had a wheelbase a further 2in shorter. Otherwise there were few changes on the later production cars although some details were changed – such as the headlamp covers, the horizontal extra air intakes and the side feature lines. Both prototype and production cars had lightweight integrated plastic bumpers, crash-proof up to speeds of 5mph.

Tail view of another prototype shows detail differences from production models – Z1 badge on the left and boot lock on the right.

The 'chassis' of the Z1 was a fully-galvanised steel monocoque. The external plastic panels were so easily replaced that to remove the entire 'body' was a half-hour job for a trained mechanic; this augured well for repairs of minor body damage. The doors disappeared downwards into very deep and wide sills which offered excellent side impact protection. The windscreen frame was actually a roll-over bar, and was designed to lead the air above the cockpit. It was also fitted with two grab handles. Another safety feature was a tubular crossmember which stiffened the scuttle structure.

Particular attention was paid to the aerodynamics. The body was shaped like a wedge, from the gently sloping front to the high, stubby tail. Following the example of the M1, the famous BMW kidneys were integrated in the front bumper, while the headlamps were set behind glass fairings. There were special aerodynamic exterior mirrors, painted in the body colour. To avoid turbulence below the car there was a smooth undershield, and the rear silencer was shaped like an upside-down aircraft wing. The result was a drag coefficient of 0.36 in closed form, or 0.43 with the soft-top down. This was achieved quite without visible aids such as wings or spoilers – which may actually have disappointed some customers!

The 2.5-litre six-cylinder engine was positioned well behind the front axle line. The McPherson strut suspension was borrowed from the 3-series without change, except for the 2in wider front track. There were new ideas at the rear: the gearbox and differential were rigidly connected by a hollow tube, described somewhat pretentiously by BMW as a 'transaxle tube' but conventionally known as a torque tube. The multi-link rear suspension was a new development and was subsequently used on the E36 3-series of 1990. The boot was nominally of almost 10cu ft (260 litres) but offered only minimal luggage space as it was mostly full of spare wheel. In any case BMW described the Z1 as a 'fun car – a contrast to the carefully developed mass-produced family saloon'. Hiding under a tonneau cover behind the seats was the folding soft-top, lined and quite waterproof, raised by hand and fitted with two catches to the windscreen frame.

The interior was simple and functional, presenting the driver with few distractions. Special bucket seats held you tightly, and instrumentation was reduced to the necessary minimum. In the best BMW tradition, controls were ergonomically well laid out. The fat-rimmed three-spoke

Simple, straight lines (top) are so functional, and do not really hint that here is a car that is an extraordinary experience to drive. The stubby tail (left) – with badge on the right – and well-integrated light clusters show attention **to aerodynamic details. The chrome button behind the door (above left) activates both window and door; the handle on the door has only an aesthetic function. Most of the boot space (above right) is taken up by the spare wheel.**

steering wheel, always on the left, felt absolutely right. The manual five-speed gearbox and the gearchange were taken from the 325i without change, and the Z1 was not available with an automatic gearbox. At 2750lb (1250kg) the Z1 was not exactly a lightweight, so performance was surprisingly good – top speed was 140mph (225kph) and 0-62mph (100kph) took 7.9sec. The 205/55VR-15 tyres stood up to centrifugal forces of 0.92G – in excess of any comparable production car. The highly effective four-wheel disc brake system was also borrowed from the normal 3-series cars.

The Z1 was only available in a limited range of standard colours – originally just red, metallic green, yellow and metallic black, but towards the end of production some cars also appeared in metallic blue or metallic purple. Apart from these, one Z1 was finished in a very non-standard colour scheme by the well-known artist A.R. Penck. This upheld BMW's tradition for creating mobile works of art, started in 1975 with a 3.0 CSL coupé. Warhol, Fuchs and Lichtenstein have all practised their art on BMW 'canvases', and in 1991 Penck decorated a red Z1 with abstract symbols.

Another new idea, at that time unique, was that BMW developed a whole range of accessories to match the car. This 'Z1 Collection' included sunglasses, luggage and clothing, and formed an important part of the marketing strategy for the car: an exclusive hand-built car needs equally exclusive ancillaries, and BMW saw the

Another in a long line of 'BMW Art' cars. This Z1 is the work of New York artist A. R. Penck. Shown at the end of 1995 but with an uncertain future, the Just 4/2 (left) is a novel concept from the BMW-Technik subsidiary in Munich.

advantage of taking this business for themselves. Besides, if you could not afford a Z1, maybe you could buy the sunglasses and still bask in the glory of the car!

Certainly, the Z1 was an image-builder for BMW, even if it is probable that the exercise was not a profitable one. The star of the 1987 Frankfurt show only went into

production almost a year later, in July 1988, when there was a list of 5000 provisional orders. At first only six cars were built per day, but this eventually grew to 18 cars per day, all manufactured in the special pre-production facility in BMW's Munich factory. Many of the original orders came from speculators hoping to make a quick profit, so actual sales were quite limited when things settled down. The problem was above all the exorbitant price of over DM 80,000, later increased to DM 89,000 – almost what you paid for an M3. The American market took fewer cars than expected, and as a result about 80 per cent of Z1 sales were in Germany. Only a tiny number came to Britain. In 1990-91, the price in the UK was £36,925.

Worse was to come. Mercedes-Benz added insult to injury by introducing its new 300SL in 1989 at a price that was only fractionally higher than the Z1. Other planned expensive sports cars, such as the Treser-VW

Although the soft-top looks a tight fit, it is surprisingly roomy under it (left). The soft-top (below left) is stowed under this hinged, rigid tonneau panel behind the seats. The boot lid (below) is very narrow, and the bonnet is hinged at the front.

roadster or the small Bitter, had disappeared without trace. The Mazda MX5 hit the market as a small and inexpensive sports car, and BMW was left high and dry with its costly rival. Sales continued to slow down, despite occasional price reductions, and in 1990 the decision was made to let production run out by the middle of the following year. Still, the production total of 8000 reached by June 1991 was well above the figure that had originally been forecast.

There is, however, no stopping the flood of new ideas from BMW-Technik, even if most of them will probably never see production. At the end of 1995, the motorcycle-inspired 'Just 4/2' appeared at the Tokyo Motor Show: this study for a simple lightweight leisure vehicle might still have a chance in the future. It was designed, incidentally, by British-born RCA graduate Robert Powell, who had previously worked for Rover and Porsche.

The Z1 on the road ....

The first impression of the Z1 is the unusual way the doors open: at the touch of a button, the side window slides down into the door, and at the same time the door disappears down into the deep leather-covered sill. At the risk of dislocating something, you swing over the sill to

glide down into the deep and hard – but not uncomfortable – bucket seat. You sit well down in the car and feel very close to the surface of the road, with the top of the closed door at shoulder level. The seating position suggests a low centre of gravity – and holds out the promise of tenacious road-holding.

Despite the flamboyant interior trim, the cockpit still feels like that of a sports car. You almost expect a full racing harness, so it is disappointing to find quite ordinary three-point seat belts. The windscreen is steeply raked, and the M3-like three-spoke steering wheel with its thick rim feels just right. There are just four simple dials on the dashboard – a 240kph (150mph) speedometer, a 7000rpm tachometer, a fuel gauge and a water temperature gauge. No trace of a glovebox, and controls for heating and ventilation have been banished to the centre console together with the radio cassette. There is, however, a lockable storage space behind the passenger seat.

Further back is the small boot, accessible from the outside through the narrow lid but also from the tonneau area when you remove a 10in deep panel behind the seats. If you leave the 'spacesaver' spare wheel at home, there is actually quite a lot of room for luggage in the boot and the tonneau – but you should leave some room for the folding soft-top. If you fill the entire space with luggage, you are obliged to drive with the soft-top up.

Z1's high 'sill' means that getting in and out is not easy – particularly when the soft-top is up! – but practice eventually makes perfect.

So far the car feels very similar to the normal 3-series, even down to the slightly cramped driving position. The same goes for the 2.5-litre engine which is highly refined and silky smooth, barely audible at idle. One might have hoped that the engine would sound a bit more aggressive, in the manner of the M3, and perhaps the acoustic engineers should have given it a more sporting note to match the undoubted power – and 170bhp is not to be sneezed at. At low revs the performance seems unexceptional, but the Z1 shows its true colours as you pass 3000rpm. At anything up to 50mph this might be any old 3-series convertible, but then the aerodynamic improvements make themselves felt and there is no stopping the Z1. A 325i eventually runs out of breath, but the Z1 keeps going on, forcing the speedometer needle past the 150mph mark.

This car is a delight to drive for any distance. In narrow, twisting lanes, the temptation is to keep the revs up, using the power to the full in the lower gears. The agility of the car fully lives up to its reputation. It goes through curves as if on rails, the slight tendency to understeer easily corrected with the direct and positive steering. The car feels very safe, as a sports car should; and unlike many sports cars, it also offers a very comfortable ride.

Of course, it is most fun to drive with the doors down – up to about 50mph. At higher speeds it gets too noisy and windy in the cockpit, so you raise the doors and windows again. One experienced Z1 driver advises that you should drive with the doors up, but with the window on the driver's side down – it is too draughty with both windows down.

Soon it dawns on you that the Z1 is not only a sports car, equally at home on the highways and byways, but also an attention getter, a style statement, a car for posing. It also has versatility in its high-speed performance and low-speed refinement, a car for city traffic and for the motorway. You cannot expect any more from what is basically a car for fun.

The Wiesmann roadster ....

However good a car is, it can always be improved on. This was the philosophy of the brothers Friedhelm and Martin Wiesmann from Dülmen in Westphalen. They set up a small company, Wiesmann Auto-Sport GmbH & Co, offering a variety of special equipment for Mercedes-Benz and Porsche, but in particular for the BMW convertibles: tailored luggage, hard-tops and so on. They offer a hard-top for the Z1, as well as other 'goodies' including air conditioning and a more powerful 210bhp 2.9-litre engine.

Not content with this, after a development period of seven years they brought out their own car with BMW mechanicals. Two roadster models were introduced in mid-1993, externally identical but with different BMW six-cylinder engines, the MF 25 with 2.5 litres and 170bhp, and the MF 35 with 3.5 litres and 211bhp. Following the example of the Z1, the cars had the engine well behind the front axle line, in the 'front-mid position'. The five-speed gearbox was from BMW but the suspension was improved with assistance from specialists such as Bilstein and Eibach. The basis of the car is a tubular spaceframe partly covered in aluminium and incorporating side impact beams. The glass-fibre body is styled along the lines of the Austin-Healey 3000. The complete front end is removable to give access to the engine.

The interior is strictly functional: a leather-covered three-spoke steering wheel, seven round dials in a leather-covered panel above the centre console, narrow doors with small wind-down windows, and a simple folding soft-top. The seating position is so low that it feels almost as if your backside scrapes the tarmac. Surprisingly there is enough room around the pedals even for drivers with large feet – unlike many other sports cars!

The boot measures 9.25cu ft (250 litres) and offers more room for luggage than the Z1 because there is no spare wheel. With a Wiesmann, you have to fall back on a puncture repair kit! The boot is actually shaped to carry a golf bag, and at the front of it is the 11-gallon (55-litre) petrol tank. There is some additional luggage space in the tonneau behind the seats.

The car is a true lightweight: the MF 25 tips the scales

A glimpse of the future. At over 50mph the 'ground-effect' underbody profile adds to stability. Driving with doors down in winter is only for hardy individuals. Never mind how cold outside, the heater is so effective that you can have the soft-top down even in the depths of winter.

at 1883lb (855kg) while the MF 35 weighs 2192lb (995kg), with overall dimensions of 153.15in (3890mm) length and 65in (1650mm) width. Claimed top speeds are 130mph (210kph) for the MF 25 and 143mph (230kph) for the MF 35. The original prices were DM 89,000 for the MF 25 and DM 99,000 for the MF 35.

With the new 3-series engines becoming available, Wiesmann changed the model line-up in January 1995. The MF 25-4 was fitted with the 24-valve 193bhp engine and the weight went up to 2192lb (995kg). The MF 35 was replaced by the new MF 3, fitted with the 286bhp 3-litre engine as well as the limited slip differential from the BMW M3. This car also put on weight, to 2313lb (1050kg). At the end of 1995 Wiesmann again changed engine availability, so that the 1996 models were the MF 28 with the 2.8-litre 193bhp engine from the 328i, and the MF 3 with the 3.2-litre 321bhp engine from the revised M3. A six-speed gearbox was an option on both cars. Top speeds increased to 140mph (225kph) and 158mph (255kph) respectively,

and 0-62mph (100kph) acceleration could be accomplished in 6.0 and 4.9sec. Prices were DM 124,900 for the MF 26 and DM 149,500 for the MF 3.

The Wiesmann roadsters combine nostalgia with elegance, and look particularly bewitching when the standard 17in wheels are replaced by optional 18in wheels. They also make the most wonderful sound which perfectly matches their breathtaking performance. Some road testers have already drawn the conclusion that the Wiesmann is the modern re-incarnation of the famed Shelby Cobra! At the time of writing about 50 cars have been sold , mostly in Germany, the most popular model being the potent MF 3.

Replicar? Front view of the Wiesmann MF 3 suggests 1950s themes. Seen from the side this glass-fibre roadster also has definite overtones of classic British designs. Rear end has some capricious detailing, quite unlike any other series production car.

STARLIGHT EXPRESS: Z3

T he Z3 Roadster was long rumoured in the press around the world, and in Germany was predicted to be a rival for the new roadsters from Mercedes-Benz and Porsche. That there was strong demand for open two-seater sports cars was something that the motor industry had long ignored. Then, suddenly, the floodgates opened, and several manufacturers produced new sports cars, like rabbits out of the magician's hat. Mazda set the trend with the MX5. The Lotus Elan with its Isuzu engine could have been a competitor but was too expensive. In 1995, the Fiat Barchetta and the MGF were introduced, and the Lotus Elise, the Renault Spyder and the Caterham 21 made their first appearance.

According to Wolfgang Reitzle, BMW's engineering director, the world-wide market for this type of car is estimated at 155,000 per year, and the main target groups for the marketing of these cars are women, young people, and those who want to re-live their youth. The idea for a small BMW sports car was born at the end of the 1980s,

The Z3 follows the traditions of BMW, as advanced in design and engineering as its ancestors were in their day. From left, forebears are 3/15 (1929-32), 315/1 (1935-36), 328 (1936-40), 507 (1956-59) and Z1 (1988-91).

while the Z1 was still in production, and the decision was made during an informal get-together of the company's board round a table in a Bavarian beer garden. The slogan which later became a seal of approval was a small roadster 'made by BMW'.

Mercedes-Benz and Porsche had already shown design studies for the sports cars they intended to introduce in 1996, but BMW, by contrast, revealed no clues about its intentions. Outsiders were not allowed to see, much less drive, the Z3 before the press launch in November 1995 and the official introduction at the Detroit Motor Show in January 1996. BMW only relented in mid-1995, when the press became vociferous and had to be satisfied with the release of a few official

Here is room to expand. The BMW factory in Spartanburg, South Carolina, is the birthplace of the Z3 – 70 per cent of the parts are made in the USA. The Z3 is engineered by BMW experience, but built by newly trained recruits. Here (below) the rear axle and transmission are married up to the rest of the car.

pictures. Meanwhile, the prototypes had completed almost a million miles on test, in conditions ranging from the boiling heat of Death Valley to the freezing cold of a Scandinavian winter. An important requirement was that the car had to be practical for everyday use. Amazingly, the car was developed over a period of only 34 months – 18 months less than any previous BMW – from the moment the styling was signed off to the start of series production, and even the pre-development styling phase took less than a year.

In fact, the Z3 was driven before introduction by one outsider, Pierce Brosnan, the actor chosen to play Agent 007 James Bond in the new *Goldeneye* film. BMW prepared two running prototypes to act in a supporting role in the film. Neither the film maker nor the car maker could have wished for better publicity. They advertised each other's product, and the result was record takings at the box office, as well as long waiting lists for BMW dealers. Actually, the Z3 is only seen on the screen for about five minutes, and in the film Bond resorts to the traditional Aston Martin DB5 for a spectacular car chase sequence against a Ferrari 355 GTS.

With the Z3, however, BMW also hit the headlines for a quite different reason. This is the first BMW car to be manufactured solely outside Germany, in BMW's new factory in the USA. In 1992 BMW bought a tract of land at Spartanburg near Greenville in recession-hit South Carolina, built an all-new factory, and hired local labour that was trained to BMW standards of building cars. However, at first BMW did not reveal what it intended to make in the new factory, causing widespread speculation – only in 1994 was it revealed that it was to be a sports car. The factory cost $600 million and has a floor area greater than the original Munich factory.

The first car – a 318i saloon – came off the Spartanburg assembly line in 1995, and the initial production target was 30 cars per day. The plant is eventually expected to produce 300 cars per day, with two-shift working, and two-thirds of the production will be Z3s. This equals an annual production of 90,000 cars, including 60,000 Z3s, but the factory can easily be expanded if there is the demand for more. There is plenty of open space around, as well as excellent communications – the freeway goes past the front door.

At first it was difficult for the new labour force to

61

Mutual back-scratching.
Pierce Brosnan as James
Bond in the film
Goldeneye had the use
of a Z3 for filming in
Costa Rica.

Works of art,
contemporary German
style: Z3 and the Berlin
Reichstag, wrapped up
by Christo.

Low seating position, low waist line and not a lot of ground clearance – this is roadster renaissance as only BMW could do it.

Z3's stubby rear end is reminiscent of some Japanese designs; the boot lid opens down to bumper level.

meet the high build quality expected of BMW cars. And besides, we are not now talking about a small series of cars built by hand: in contrast to previous BMW sports cars, the Z3 is a mass-production vehicle. An army of BMW production engineers was posted from Munich to supervise the processes. The workers are divided into teams, members take turns to act as team leaders, and

before each shift hold discussions about the work which lies ahead. Parts are delivered to the factory on the 'just in time' principle, and many parts are sourced locally from suppliers who have set up their own plants in the neighbourhood – the Canadian firm Magna, for instance, has set up a subsidiary factory at Greenville to stamp out Z3 body panels.

Evidently there is a great deal of local pride in the enterprise – the feeling is that BMW chose South Carolina because of the traditional craftmanship in the area. The Spartanburg factory is in some ways very different from BMW's German factories: all employees

63

wear the same workwear and everybody is on first-name terms – very unusual by German standards! It helps everybody to feel part of the team but also shows the influence from Japanese work practices. The factory is split into four sections and currently employs 1000 people, but the workforce will grow to 1500-2000 as production builds up to the maximum capacity.

And what of the car? The compact, muscular Z3 seems very much to be 'made in Germany', apart, perhaps, from the use of plastic materials for the interior. Compared with its immediate predecessor, the Z3 is emotive where the Z1 was innovative. The Z3, known in the factory as E36/7, is described as sporting, distinctive, purist – and affordable. This was an important part of the concept – which perhaps inevitably led to some compromises – but the result is that the Z3 sells in Germany for DM 43,700 for the base 1.8-litre model or DM 48,700 for the more powerful and better equipped 1.9-litre version (prices which translate to £19,400 and £21,600 at early 1996 exchange rates). When the car was launched to the press at Spartanburg in November 1995 and these prices were mentioned, even the most hard-boiled scribbler joined in the spontaneous round of applause. By comparison, the cheapest BMW convertible model, the 318i, costs DM 54,800 in Germany. Perhaps BMW has made a competitor for its own cars…

The Z3 only resembles the rest of the BMW family from the front, and even here there are distinctive differences. Following the presentation of several different design proposals, the favoured one had a huge clamshell bonnet sloping down to the bumper at the front, and a short cut-off rear end. The rear is not traditional BMW except for the badge in the centre, the light clusters give the tail panel a distinctive shape, and the obligatory high-level brake light sits in a recess on the boot lid. The front end is longer than is normal these days and the windscreen relatively upright – it is not a particularly aerodynamic design and the drag coefficient of 0.40 is unsurprising. Where the Z1 was a functional design of straight lines, the Z3 has a rounded, organic shape. The wheelbase is long relative to the short overall length, the track is wide, there are hardly any overhangs, the wheelarches are enormous, and the whole car is pulled tight down over the wheels.

There are naturally some of the expected BMW signatures in the design, such as the double kidney grille and the four round headlamps behind glass fairings, while the admittedly non-functional air vents behind the front wheelarches are directly inspired by the classic 507. The cockpit borrows heavily from the BMW parts bin, with

instruments and controls just like those you find in a 3-series. There is perhaps a contrast between the highly stylised exterior and the much more functional interior, but all the expected fittings and equipment are there, possibly to the disappointment of old-school sports car drivers who may prefer a more spartan environment.

The narrow bucket seats with integral headrests are a new design, specially developed for the Z3. There is plenty of stowage space in the interior, including a glovebox in the dashboard and a lockable cubbyhole behind the seats. The optional stereo system fits into this space behind the driver.

The soft-top is as simple as you would expect it on a real sports car. Made from unlined fabric (polyacryl and cotton), it is simply fixed to the windscreen frame with two catches. Releasing these catches and pushing back the soft-top allows it to fold up neatly behind the seats, where it is stowed under a tonneau cover. It is also an effective soft-top: every single Z3 undergoes a comprehensive water test in the factory.

The body is of unitary construction, the inner structure is galvanised and all skin panels are bolted on. The weight of 2533lb (1150kg) reflects the passive safety features, including deformable zones front and rear, side impact protection, and a windscreen frame that doubles as a roll-over bar. Unlike the 3-series convertible, there is no automatic rear roll-over bar to emerge if the car should roll over. However, the Z3 has ABS and double airbags as standard, while a traction control system is optional on the 1.9-litre version.

Then there is the 7cu ft (180 litres) boot behind the rear axle, and immediately above the axle is the 11-gallon (51 litres) fuel tank. Because space was limited, it was impossible to fit the new multi-link rear suspension from the current 3-series (E36), so the Z3 – like the 3-series Compact – uses the trailing arm rear suspension from the previous 3-series (E30). In fact, of all the models in the present 3-series, it is the Compact which has most in common with the Z3. The power-assisted rack and pinion steering is used by both cars, although it is higher geared in the Z3. The McPherson strut front suspension is straight from the 3-series parts bin. The wheels are of 15in diameter, with Michelin tyres.

Steel wheels are standard on the 1.8-litre, but the 1.9-

Wet road, tight bends – not a problem. The Z3 is designed for safety. There are some unusual colour combinations (inset) – appropriate for such a trend-setting car. Interior is familiar from the 3-series but the upholstery is more unusual. There are plenty of stowage spaces.

The eight-valve 1.8-litre engine comes from the BMW 318i and produces 115bhp.

litre gets alloy wheels. With lowered suspension and a shorter wheelbase than the Compact, the Z3 proves to be an entirely good-natured car with terrific handling. Its behaviour reminds you of the first M3, the hottest version of the previous 3-series. The five-speed gearbox is also an old friend, the normal Getrag 'box from the 3-series, but the bigger-engined Z3 can be fitted with an optional automatic four-speed gearbox.

It was never proposed that the Z3 should be mid-engined, as the MGF, or that it should have front-wheel drive, as the Fiat Barchetta. A BMW must have a classic powertrain: longitudinal front engine and rear-wheel drive. The Z3 is fitted with a choice of two engines: the 115bhp 1.8-litre eight-valve 'four' from the 318i or the marginally bored-out 318is 16-valve unit with an impressive 140bhp from its 1.9 litres. A few other changes were made from the 318is engine, thus the original plain cam followers were replaced by roller-type cam followers, with the benefits of less friction, better economy and longer engine life. Both engines are built in BMW's Austrian engine factory at Steyr, and both meet the strictest current emission control standards. It might just be a coincidence that the engine sizes are so close to those of the Mazda MX5...

Both Z3 versions are quick: the 1.9-litre shaves 1sec off the 0-62mph (0-100kph) time of 10.5sec for the 1.8-litre, and top speeds are respectively 127mph (205kph) and 120mph (194kph) – in other words well up there with the once breathtaking performance of the classic 507. To extend a Z3 to the full, you need to drive it on

Germany's unrestricted *Autobahns*, rather than the American freeways with their much lower speed limits. However, the Z3 is as much intended to be enjoyed on minor roads, with the soft-top down, when you are not in a hurry to finish the journey.

Should you find that you want something extra to personalise your Z3, BMW has a long list of options. There are 17in wheels, or cast alloy wheels in both 16in and 17in sizes, and even a chrome package for the front wing air vents, outside and inside door handles, side window frames, tread panels and instrument bezels. Other possibilities are a rigid tonneau cover in body colour, wind deflectors, a hard-top, a roll-over cage, leather upholstery and an automatic gearbox. There is a wide choice of colour combinations too, with the solid colours black, bright red, purple, dark green, turquoise and white, and metallic shades of silver, black, two blues and two greens.

Like Mercedes-Benz with the C-class, BMW offers four different Z3 option packages which can be supplied individually or combined. The 'comfort' package includes electric windows, powered soft-top, automatic gearbox, air conditioning, cruise control, heated seats, hard-top and wind deflectors. The 'exclusive' package offers a variety of special colour options with a wood-and-leather interior. The 'tradition' package combines the interior wood trim with a wood-rim steering wheel, the chrome fittings, spoke-type alloy wheels and a chrome luggage rack with suitcase. Finally, the 'sport' package provides alternative sports seats, lowered

The 16-valve 1.9-litre engine is new in the BMW programme, this 140bhp unit making its debut in the Z3.

suspension, a limited slip differential, 17in wheels and aerodynamic aids.

We can soon also expect to see more powerful versions of the Z3. Although it is a tight fit, BMW's six-cylinder engine will just squeeze under the bonnet. The M Roadster, the ultimate 'pocket rocket', is expected to go on sale at the end of 1996. Under its long bonnet, this Z3 derivative hides the engine from the current M3, the 3.2-litre six-cylinder unit with twin overhead camshafts, four valves per cylinder and the 'Vanos' variable valve timing system. There are six individual ignition coils and the most up-to-date electronic engine management system. Together with this engine comes the new BMW sequential six-speed gearbox.

This version was developed by the BMW M GmbH – BMW's motor sport department. The exterior has also been modified, with much wider rear wings and a deeper front spoiler. Both track and wheels are wider: front rims are 7.5in wide, rear rims no less than 8.5in. The suspension has been tuned to match the performance and the braking system comes from the M3. Four chromed tailpipes distinguish the rear view, although the exhaust system has been tuned for quietness rather than performance, so the M Roadster has 'only' 315bhp as opposed to the 321bhp of the M3. It still covers 0-62mph (100kph) in 5.8sec and the top speed has been electronically limited to 155mph (250kph) – without the limiter the theoretical maximum would be closer to 170mph (275kph). As it is still a relative lightweight, the fuel consumption averages 33.6mpg (8.4 L/100km).

The interior features extra equipment and is more luxurious. There is two-tone leather upholstery, and a special leather-covered three-spoke steering wheel with integrated switchgear. The instruments have chrome bezels and now include dials for oil pressure and oil temperature, as well as a clock. There are special oval door mirrors and the front wing gills have been redesigned, although appearances still deceive and they are no more functional than on the ordinary Z3. The M Roadster was previewed at the Geneva Motor Show in March 1996 and was expected to cost around DM 78,000 (approximately £35,000), which would put it on a par, price-wise, with the new Porsche Boxster. Incidentally, at the Geneva show the Z3 was chosed as 'cabriolet of the year' by an international jury.

Tuning specialists have also been quick to adopt the Z3 and already offer a variety of improvements. One of the best-known BMW specialists, A. C. Schnitzer of Aachen, introduced an engine conversion for the 1.8-litre base model in March 1996. A capacity increase to 2.1 litres results in 130bhp at 5000rpm and torque of 200Nm at 3000rpm. Because the two-valve engine is more flexible and offers more torque at lower revs, this version of the Z3 will accelerate from 0-62mph (100kph) in 9.5sec, and reaches a top speed of 130mph (210kph); the conversion costs DM 9950. The Hamann company of Hüttisheim launched its own 'M Roadster' in April 1996: the 350 Roadster has an M3 engine tuned to 350bhp, a top speed of 175mph (282kph), and 0-62mph (100kph) acceleration in 4.9sec. The car is fitted with

Same style, different periods: rounded shapes of new BMW and old Mack trucks. The surprisingly large plastic rear window can be zipped out of the soft-top fabric.

height-adjustable suspension and costs DM 119,800.

Also expected from BMW itself, probably at the end of 1996 or early in 1997, is the normal six-cylinder version of the Z3, with the 2.8-litre engine, well-known from the 328i version of the 3-series. This engine develops 193bhp at 5300rpm with maximum torque of 280Nm at 3950rpm. The Z3 2.8-litre will feature small changes to the exterior and the chassis to match the bigger engine. And what of a V8-engined Z3? Rumours are circulating but BMW continues to deny them…

At the same time prototypes of three/four-seater Z3-based fastback coupés are being tested, already fitted with the more comfortable rear suspension from the old M3. With the enthusiastic reception given to the new Alfa Romeo GTV coupé and the sensational arrival of the Audi TT, there is a strong possibility of a new racing series for such cars. A Z3 coupé would fit right in there, and could even become a challenger in the touring car championship.

The 1.9-litre Z3 has some of the 'goodies' fitted as standard – but big cast alloy wheels and wide tyres are an extra-cost option.

The Z3 on the road..........................

The day is overcast, only now and then does the sun penetrate the clouds. It is not too cold, not too hot – just the right weather to go for a spin in the new Z3.

The car sits low on the road. The double headlamps behind their shapely lenses seem to wink at you – is there a promise here? Of the different versions, I have chosen

Meatier front spoiler
instantly identifies the
M Roadster, a 3.2-litre
version revealed as a
prototype at the 1996
Geneva Show and
planned for production
from late 1996. Interior
upgrades include chrome-
rimmed instruments,
extra dials on the centre
console, sportier seats
and adventurous colour
combinations.

Discreet badges on boot lid and front wing grilles are clues, but flared rear wheelarches are a more obvious hint that the 315bhp M Roadster will be the ultimate Z3.

to start with the base model, which from the outside differs from the more expensive versions only in its wheels. The proportions of the two-seater are chunky, with a wide stance, and the soft-top fits so tightly that it seems almost indecent. It seems a much bigger car than the Mazda MX5, but is in fact a mere 2in longer.

The fact that the Z3 is a car of contrasts cannot be disregarded – contrasts between the playful design cues of the exterior and the soberly functional interior that is expected from BMW. These two elements both complement and fight against each other. Externally, the door handle at least is perhaps unexpectedly functional – unlike the concealed push-button release handle of the 507 which lives again on the Fiat Barchetta. But those gills on the front wings lead you to expect other retro features or design jokes, yet the interior is devoid of any similar cues – there is not even any painted metal.

The Z3's cabin, of course, is well-planned and well-made, ergonomically correct and very comfortable. The ambience is familiar, but plain and unsophisticated. It is an interior built to the BMW philosophy of 'driving pleasure' – rather than 'design pleasure' – and it lives up to the expectations of the marque. But anyone dissatisfied with this can always pay extra for the chrome and wood trim package to add a touch of decadence to the starkly functional flavour.

The word 'roadster' appears on the tread plate of the door sill. The seats, almost as low as the sills, are not exactly thickly padded but have electric motors for both height and front-rear adjustment. The low seating position gives a feeling of security – you almost feel the low centre of gravity. The seat belts run through brackets on the side of the integral headrests which saves fumbling around for them, and the seat belt locks are also integrated in the seats. The windscreen is at just about the right distance, and beyond it is the long curving bonnet, drawing the eye out to the horizon. The unlined soft-top still leaves more than adequate headroom; even a driver well over 6ft has a few inches clearance above the top of the head. The instruments, living under a deep cowl, comprise just four round dials, as normal with a BMW: a 155mph (240kph) speedometer, a 7000rpm tachometer and smaller fuel and water temperature gauges. Nothing to distract the driver! On the other hand the standard equipment includes such refinements as central locking and electrically adjustable exterior mirrors, but the windows have to be wound up and down by hand.

The fairly large three-spoke steering wheel has no adjustment but falls well to hand for most drivers, and the familiar 3-series gear lever is so well-positioned that it almost jumps into your hand. The engine note sounds rather restrained and only a soft murmur escapes: this is, after all, a politically correct engine, quiet as well as clean! The gear lever has short and precise movements; the power-assisted rack and pinion steering is light. I accelerate, change up the 'box – but the real pleasure is waiting at the first bend. The car feels solid as a rock, it corners completely flat, and there is no rattle, shake or roll. And when the corners get tighter, it turns out that the Z3 has considerable reserves to draw on. The limitation here is the 1.8-litre engine: the car is under-powered, the engine feeling hard pressed as you keep your foot on the floor.

Up to about 90mph you can tolerate the noise in the car with the soft-top up, but then noise from the wind, road and engine combine to create background music louder than a disco. I leave the highway and take to the minor roads that wind up into the mountains – but first I need some fresh air and stop to get the soft-top out of the way. The brakes are superb: unlike the Compact, nothing was compromised on the Z3 brakes, which are discs on all four wheels. Only James Bond's Z3 is fitted with a parachute for extra stopping power!

Only two catches need to be released to free the soft-top: a light push and it almost folds up on its own,

disappearing into the recess behind the seats where there is also an easily accessible, lockable cubby hole. The soft-top cover, stored in the boot when not in use, is a semi-rigid plastic cover which has to be attached with four press studs. This can be difficult without practice – although easier to deal with than the MX5 soft-top cover. A permanently fitted rigid cover, as found on the Barchetta or the Z1, would be an improvement. The boot is very roomy: the battery sits in the engine compartment and the 'spacesaver' spare wheel is in a separate compartment below the boot.

With the soft-top down, you appreciate the small fixed triangular side windows which protect the passengers from the worst of the wind buffeting, even when the main side windows are wound down. Now you can really enjoy chasing those bends. You pick a line and the Z3 sticks to it. The car always feel good-natured and completely safe. It proves able to cope with even greater cornering forces than the Z1. The handling is well balanced and neutral, a cross between initial slight understeer and, if you lift off in the middle of the curve, mild oversteer that is easily corrected. The Z3 is always obedient and faithful and never bites back at you. Even in the wet you can chuck this car around with impunity – and if the passenger starts to complain you remind him that, if the worst comes to the worst, he has a perfectly good airbag. Incidentally, a sensor in the passenger seat ensures that this airbag only goes off if the seat is occupied in a crash.

Changing over to the 16-valve 1.9-litre model is like entering another world. On paper it is not so very different from the 1.8 – but compared subjectively it

The simple trailing arm rear suspension from the 3-series Compact, plus a space-saver spare wheel under the boot, help to give the Z3 a reasonably large boot.

Country roads are the best place to take the Z3 for a spin. With a range of 370 miles from the 11-gallon tank, you can feel as free as a bird.

This car has an automatic gearbox as well as the luxurious wood-and-leather interior package (left). A lockable storage compartment continues the centre console (below); note also the special seat belt guide bracket at the top of the seat.

seems to go like a rocket, sounds like Joe Cocker and offers more thrills than a ride at Disneyland. It can do everything the 1.8 can do, and then some. This engine develops awesome power even at low revs, with bags of torque. If you feel like it, you can drive everywhere in top without the engine seeming the slightest bit bothered. You never have the feeling that the 1.9-litre is under pressure because there is always some extra power available. This model also spoils you with its better equipment.

You realise that this is the car for the real sports car enthusiast who wants to drive fast and furiously, exploring the limits of car and driver – by contrast the

1.8-litre model is more for those who enjoy cruising about in an open car and who rarely use the performance to the full. The 1.9-litre moves briskly and makes a sound to rival the M3.

This is a stunningly competent car, with reserves that will probably never be explored by most of its owners. Its ideal weight distribution and low centre of gravity ensure dynamics that exceed those of any BMW saloon car by a considerable margin. The car is stable, the body

The almost endless list of extra-cost options can add considerably to the price of a Z3. This car is fitted with the 'chrome' package – obvious from the bright windscreen frame and trimmed front wing grilles.

movements well controlled. With a firm grip on the leather-covered steering wheel, you wait for the next bend and fling the car into it, hardly lifting the foot from the pedal – and are rewarded by protesting squeals from the tyres. Much has changed since the days of the classics but this Z3 offers just as much driver involvement as the roadsters of old.

Finally I come back to earth with a bump, trying a 1.9-litre Z3 with the automatic gearbox. Still, you can select either sports or economy modes, and also change manually between gears, so you can hold the car in low gear – useful on slippery roads. But the Z3 engine and the auto 'box are not well matched, this car really needing a more powerful six-cylinder engine. It is still fine for cruising and will probably suit many Z3 customers very well – after all the automatic version is mainly intended for the convenience of American drivers who are expected to buy fully half of the production run.

ROADSTERS AND CONVERTIBLES TODAY

The fact that open cars of any sort are always more collectable than saloons is clearly demonstrated by the higher prices they attract. With some classic cars, there are now fewer closed than open survivors, many saloons and coupés having been broken up for spares. And it is always the soft-top classics that get all the attention when they appear in public.

As the iron curtain was lifted at the beginning of the 1990s, suddenly there was a 'new' influx of pre-war classics that sometimes changed hands at bargain prices. However, many of them turned out to be much-modified from original, and some were downright forgeries. This was particularly the case for some re-appearing BMW 328s which in top condition are now worth at least DM 300,000 (£130,000) in Germany. This sort of money tempted certain 'restorers' to fit recreated 328 bodies on chassis from the lesser 315 or 319 models. Let the buyer beware! Common sense suggests that verification is called for, with the help of BMW clubs or the company's archive department in Munich, to ensure that the chassis number of a particular car is not already spoken for. There are an estimated 200-plus surviving 328s, most of them in Germany.

Demand for the more ordinary pre-war six-cylinder cars is at a less hectic level. Cabriolets and roadsters with the blue and white logo appear at classic car events around the world. Some are still used in historic racing, including some of the right-hand drive Frazer Nash versions sold in Britain. These are rare but are not considered any more valuable than 'ordinary' BMWs. It is only possible to guess at the number of preserved pre-war BMWs, but it must be around 1000 of the six-cylinder models, from 303 to 335 (apart from the 328s), as well as several thousand of the four-cylinder cars, from DA1 to AM4.

The BMW-supported one-make clubs can help with any information that is required, reprinted spare parts lists or workshop manuals are freely available, and many spare parts have been remanufactured. Parts and literature can also be found at the big autojumbles – at Beaulieu in Britain, Hershey in the USA, or at the German classic car shows in Mannheim or Essen. But do not be tempted to fall for a potential bargain without taking expert advice.

The most sought-after post-war open BMWs are the 507 and the 503 convertible, although there is a great difference in their respective values. From new the 503 was the more expensive car, yet is now worth only half as much as a 507. Even in middling condition, a 507 can cost around DM 400,000 (over £175,000) in Germany. Buying a car with poor bodywork requires considerable caution: all-aluminium construction means that restoration becomes very expensive, few new panels are available, and there are no common body parts with the contemporary BMW saloons. But the fact that the mechanicals are at least shared with other models makes life a little easier. World-wide there are around 100 503 convertibles and some 240 507s still in existence, most of them in Germany, Switzerland or the USA.

It is quite common to modify these cars, for instance by fitting the later, more developed and more powerful 160bhp engine from the 3200 Super. The only external difference is the stud pattern for the cylinder heads. This conversion does not significantly reduce the value of the car in question.

When it comes to the convertible versions of the 501 or 502, the rare Authenrieth-bodied cars are most sought after, and there are some instances where original saloons have had their roofs chopped to become replicas of the Baur four-door convertible. Such cars can usually be recognised by their different appearance at the top of the rear door pillar.

The compact convertibles from the 02-series (type 114) and the early 3-series (types E21 and E30) are slowly acquiring classic status. The full convertibles based on the early 02-cars are already sought-after, especially as they suffered badly from rust and many have been scrapped. Many enthusiasts are learning to appreciate the virtues of the comfortable Baur targa cabriolet versions with their

The complete restoration of a classic takes time – and money! – but pays off if the car is an original 328.

Many re-manufactured parts, such as these 507 grilles (above), are now available from specialists. A 507 can only be fitted with the particular hard-top **(above right) supplied with it when new. The owner of this 507 (right) has installed the more powerful – but similar – 160bhp engine from the BMW 3200 Super.**

overtones of the long extinct landaulet – and it is possible to speculate that, in the fullness of time, the current four-door E36 with the Baur conversion will also become a valued collector's piece. By contrast, the later convertible versions of the E30 second-generation 3-series are still considered everyday cars.

The Z1 has long had a high-tech image and is now clearly beginning to appreciate in value. Interest in this

There was never a fully convertible version of the first 3-series (E21), but specialists such as the Lumma company can chop the roof off.

BMW did not offer so many extras for the Z1 as it does the Z3 – but specialists have stepped into the breach with improvements.

car is likely to increase further now that the Z3 has been given such a positive reception. The days are long gone when a Z1 would be given away for less than DM 50,000 (£22,000) and it is a safe bet that prices will go up – although as yet all BMWs later than the 1950s are too recent to be considered in investment terms. But then most of these later cars are perfectly practical as everyday transport, parts are easily available, and there is a lively club scene.

It is rather different when we come to converted or modified cars, such as the after-market cabriolets based on the 02 or later cars. They are just as much fun as the normal factory convertibles but are likely to have depreciated much more when you come to sell them. Most enthusiasts for the classic open BMWs want originality, and want a car with a documented history – otherwise they might just as well stick with a cheaper and less exclusive marque! Collectors are also unimpressed with cars which have been in any way customised – anyone daring to turn up at a BMW club event in a metallic colour 02 with white leather upholstery and wide wheels is likely to be sent packing.

APPENDIX

Options and extras..........................

Before the war, BMW itself did not offer much in the way of extras. It was left to outside specialists who were prepared to meet every requirement – some of these companies were not normally engaged in the motor business and were content with small runs or one-offs.

By the time BMW had introduced the big V8s of the 1950s and 1960s, the company was also determined to generate extra income by offering all sorts of extras and accessories – tailored luggage, reversing lamps, fog lamps, expensive radios, special seats, leather upholstery, tow bars and a choice of rear axle ratios. Hard-tops, however, were not offered, whether for the 501/502 convertibles or for the 503. Today wood rimmed steering wheels are very popular but none of these are original. Not original either – but at least functional – are the 507-style front wing air vents that have been fitted by some 503 owners.

Almost perfect 507 can be improved with fitted luggage.

There was no hard-top option for the first 02 convertible; BMW only offered this for the second generation 3-series. They were actually beaten to the marketplace by the Wiesmann company, which also offers a Z1 hard-top – and much else besides. Numerous independent specialists quickly jumped on the bandwagon and tempted customers with an enormous variety of custom parts or technical modifications. Now BMW offers all sort of extras and accessories through its dealer network: the most popular items are wood veneer panels for dashboards, twin exhaust systems – and the famous tri-colour M-badge.

A few 503s now have 507-style front wing grilles.

Technical specifications....................

BMW 328 (1936–40)
Engine In-line six-cylinder **Construction** Cast iron block, light alloy cylinder head **Crankshaft** Four main bearings **Bore × stroke** 66mm × 96mm (2.60in × 3.78in) **Capacity** 1971cc (120.28 cu in) **Valves** Side camshaft with Duplex chain drive, overhead valves in V-form, inlet valves operated by push-rods and rockers, exhaust valves with additional cross push-rods **Compression ratio** 7.5:1 **Fuel system** Three Solex downdraught carburettors type 30JF **Maximum power** 80bhp at 5000rpm **Maximum torque** Not available **Transmission** ZF or Hurth four-speed manual gearbox, synchromesh on third and fourth, floor change **Final drive ratio** 3.70:1 or 3.88:1 **Top gear mph per 1000rpm** Not available **Chassis/body** Tubular chassis frame with box section crossmembers, body panelled partly in steel, partly in aluminium **Brakes** Hydraulic drums front and rear, mechanical handbrake on rear wheels **Front suspension** Independent with lower wishbones and upper transverse leaf spring, hydraulic shock absorbers **Rear suspension** Live axle, semi-elliptic leaf springs, hydraulic shock absorbers **Steering** Rack and pinion **Wheels/tyres** Centre-lock steel disc wheels, 3.25×16 rims with 5.25-16 tyres or 3.50×16 rims with 5.50-16 tyres **Length** 153.5in (3900mm) **Wheelbase** 94.5in (2400mm) **Width** 61in (1550mm) **Height** 55.1in (1400mm) **Front track** 45.4in (1153mm) **Rear track** 48in (1220mm) **Unladen weight** 1828lb (830kg) **Gross vehicle weight** 2687lb (1220kg) **Top speed** 93mph (150kph) **0-62mph (0-100kph)** 10.5sec **Typical fuel consumption** 19.5mpg (14.5 L/100km)

BMW 507 (1955–59)
Engine Eight cylinders in vee **Construction** Aluminium cylinder block and heads, wet cylinder steel liners **Crankshaft** Five main bearings **Bore × stroke** 82mm × 75mm (3.23in × 2.95in) **Capacity** 3168cc (193.32cu in) **Valves** Central camshaft with Duplex chain drive, in-line overhead valves operated by push-rods and rockers **Compression ratio** 7.8:1 **Fuel system** Two twin-choke Zenith downdraught carburettors type 32 NDIX **Maximum power** 150bhp at 5000rpm **Maximum torque** 174lb ft (24mkg) at 4000rpm **Transmission** ZF four-speed gearbox, fully synchronised, floor change **Final drive ratio** 3.70:1 standard; 3.42:1 or 3.90:1 optional **Top gear mph per 1000rpm** 21.4mph (34.4kph) with 3.70:1 final drive **Chassis/body** Box section frame with tubular crossmembers, all aluminium body panels **Brakes** Hydraulic brakes in Alfin drums, servo assisted; some cars experimentally fitted with front disc brakes **Front suspension** Independent with double wishbones and longitudinal torsion bars, anti-roll bar, telescopic shock absorbers **Rear suspension** Live axle, central A-bracket location and Panhard rod, longitudinal torsion bars, telescopic shock absorbers **Steering** Quadrant rack and pinion **Wheels/tyres** Centre-lock steel disc wheels, 4.50×16 rims with 6.00H-16 tyres **Length** 172.4in (4380mm) **Wheelbase** 97.6in (2480mm) **Width** 65in (1650mm) **Height** 51.2in (1300mm) **Front**

track 56.9in (1445mm) **Rear track** 56.1in (1425mm) **Unladen weight** 2819-2930lb (1280-1330kg) **Top speed** 127mph (205kph) with standard final drive; alternatively 118mph (190kph) or 137mph (220kph) **0-62mph (0-100kph)** 9-10sec **Typical fuel consumption** 16.6mpg (17 L/100km)

BMW Z1 (1988-91)
Engine In-line six-cylinder, type M20 **Construction** Cast iron cylinder block, aluminium head; engine canted over at 20° to the right **Crankshaft** Seven main bearings **Bore × stroke** 84mm × 75mm (3.31in × 2.95in) **Capacity** 2494cc (152.19 cu in) **Valves** Single overhead camshaft, belt drive, two valves per cylinder in 44° V-form **Compression ratio** 8.8:1 **Fuel system** Digital electronic fuel injection, system Bosch Motronic **Maximum power** 170bhp at 5800rpm **Maximum torque** 160.45lb ft (22.2mkg) at 4300rpm **Transmission** ZF five-speed gearbox, fully synchronised, floor change **Final drive ratio** 3.64:1 **Top gear mph per 1000rpm** 23.4mph (37.7kph) **Chassis/body** Monocoque underbody of galvanised steel, plastic body panels **Brakes** Hydraulic disc brakes front and rear, dual circuits, servo and Bosch ABS **Front suspension** Independent with McPherson struts and lower wishbones, coil springs, telescopic shock absorbers and anti-roll bar **Rear suspension** Independent multi-link suspension with coil springs, telescopic shock absorbers and anti-roll bar **Steering** Rack and pinion with power assistance **Wheels/tyres** Cast alloy wheels, 7.5J×16 rims, tyres 225/45ZR-16 (alternatively 205/55VR-15 on 7.5J×15 wheels) **Length** 154.4in (3921mm) **Wheelbase** 96.3in (2447mm) **Width** 66.5in (1690mm) **Height** 50.3in (1277mm) **Front track** 57.3in (1455mm) **Rear track** 57.9in (1470mm) **Unladen weight** 2753lb (1250kg) **Gross vehicle weight** 3216lb (1460kg) **Top speed** 140mph (225kph) **0-62mph (0-100kph)** 7.9sec **Typical fuel consumption** 24-28mpg (10-12 L/100km)

BMW Z3 1.8 litre (from 1996, chassis numbers from LA 14000)
Engine In-line four-cylinder, type M43 **Construction** Cast iron cylinder block, aluminium head **Crankshaft** Five main bearings **Bore × stroke** 84mm × 81mm (3.31in × 3.19in) **Capacity** 1796cc (109.60cu in) **Valves** Single overhead camshaft, belt driven, two valves per cylinder in V-form activated by roller-type cam followers and mushroom tappets **Compression ratio** 9.7:1 **Fuel system** Digital electronic fuel injection, system Bosch Motronic **Maximum power** 115bhp (PS) (85kW) at 5500rpm **Maximum torque** 168 Nm (124lb ft) at 3900rpm **Transmission** Fully synchronised ZF five-speed gearbox, floor change **Final drive ratio** 3.45:1 **Top gear mph per 1000rpm** 20.6mph (33.2kph) **Chassis/body** Unitary construction all-steel bodywork **Brakes** Hydraulic, ventilated disc brakes front and rear, dual circuits, servo and Teves ABS **Front suspension** Independent, McPherson struts and lower wishbones, coil springs, telescopic shock absorbers and anti-roll bar **Rear suspension** Independent with trailing arms and coil springs, telescopic shock absorbers and anti-roll bar **Steering** Rack and pinion with power assistance **Wheels/tyres** Steel disc wheels, 6.50J×15 rims with 205/60HR-15 tyres **Length** 158.5in (4025mm) **Wheelbase** 96.3in (2446mm) **Width** 66.6in (1692mm) **Height** 50.7in (1288mm) **Front track** 55.6in (1411mm) **Rear track** 56.2in (1427mm) **Unladen weight** 2533lb (1150kg) **Gross vehicle weight** 3084lb (1400kg) **Top speed** 120.5mph (194kph) **0-62mph (0-100kph)** 10.5sec **Typical fuel consumption** EC average 36.2mpg (7.8 L/100km)

BMW Z3 1.9 litre (from 1996, chassis numbers from LA 59000)
As for 1.8 litre, except: **Engine** Type M44 **Bore × stroke** 85mm ×

83.5mm (3.35in × 3.29in) **Capacity** 1895cc (115.64cu in) **Valves** Twin overhead camshafts, chain driven, four valves per cylinder **Compression ratio** 10.0:1 **Maximum power** 140bhp (PS) (103kW) at 6000rpm **Maximum torque** 180 Nm (133lb ft) at 4300rpm **Transmission** Four-speed automatic gearbox optional **Final drive ratio** 4.44:1 with automatic gearbox **Wheels/tyres** Cast alloy wheels, 7.00J×15 rims with 205/60VR-15 tyres (other wheel/tyre sizes optional) **Front track** 55.6-56in (1411-1423mm) depending on wheels/tyres **Rear track** 56.2-56.7in (1427-1439mm) depending on wheels/tyres **Unladen weight** 2588lb (1175kg) manual, 2665lb (1210kg) automatic **Gross vehicle weight** 3139lb (1425kg) manual, 3216lb (1460kg) automatic **Top speed** 127.4mph (205kph) manual, 121.8mph (196kph) automatic **0-62mph (0-100kph)** 9.5sec manual, 10.5sec automatic **Typical fuel consumption** EC average 35.3mpg (8.0 L/100km) manual, 32.5mpg (8.7 L/100km) automatic

BMW Z3 2.8 litre (from 1996)
Complete data not available at the time of publication. As 1.8/1.9 litre except: **Engine** In-line six-cylinder **Construction** Aluminium block and head **Crankshaft** Seven main bearings **Bore × stroke** 84mm × 84mm (3.31in × 3.31in) **Capacity** 2793cc (170.44cu in) **Valves** Two overhead camshafts, chain driven, four valves per cylinder in 39.5° V-form **Compression ratio** 10.2:1 **Maximum power** 193bhp (PS) (142kW) at 5300rpm **Maximum torque** 280Nm (206.5lb ft) at 3950rpm **Unladen weight** 2753lb (1250kg) **Top speed** 145mph (234kph) **0-62mph (0-100kph)** 7.5sec

BMW M Roadster (from 1996)
Model introduced at Geneva Motor Show, March 1996. Complete data not available at the time of publication. As Z3 2.8 litre except: **Bore × stroke** 86.4mm × 91mm (3.40in × 3.58in) **Capacity** 3201cc (195.34cu in) **Compression ratio** 11.3:1 **Maximum power** 315bhp (PS) (231kW) at 7200rpm **Maximum torque** 350Nm (258lb ft) at 3250rpm **Transmission** Six-speed gearbox **Wheels/tyres** Cast alloy wheels, 7.5J×17 front, 8.5J×17 rear; front tyres 225/45ZR-17, rear tyres 245/40ZR-17 **Unladen weight** 2863lb (1300kg) **Top speed** limited to 155mph (250kph) **0-62mph (0-100kph)** 5.8sec **Typical fuel consumption** EC average 33.6mpg (8.4 L/100km)

Production figures ....

Although there have been many serious BMW histories published, especially in Germany, there are still discrepancies in the published production figures. This particularly affects the pre-war models, not least because so many different coachbuilders made cabriolet or roadster bodies for cars delivered by BMW in chassis form, and some cars were even re-bodied at the time.

For the 315/1 and the 319/1, production figures are usually quoted as 242 and 102 cars respectively, although it cannot be established that these figures are correct. The uncertainty is worse with the 328 – in various books the production figure has been quoted as 461, 462 or 467 cars. The basis for the figures which follow are the original BMW car production records, in so far as these are available. Any cars not bodied by (or for) BMW have been excluded. Frazer Nash-BMW cars fitted with bodywork in Britain have also had to be excluded.

Different figures have also been quoted for the post-war models. This is hardly surprising in the case of the 501 and 502. Apart from Baur and Authenrieth, there were so many different coachbuilders in Germany and Switzerland who worked on these chassis, for which no individual production figures are known. The author has been greatly helped by the 501/502 experts in the German BMW clubs, and also by Henning Zaiss, a leading expert on Authenrieth. The figure of 252 cars for the 507 seems realistic, if we add the one-off Loof prototype. It is not now possible to be certain whether there were other prototypes without normal chassis numbers, or whether, as rumour has it, more cars were built up from spare parts after production had officially stopped.

In this book, production figures are quoted (or corrected) for the first time for the Baur targa cabriolet version of the first 3-series (the E21 model), thanks to Baur releasing the necessary information. Included in the figures are the conversions for South Africa, Greece and Jordan. There are again contradictions in the previously published figures for the BMW-built full convertible version of the E30 (second-generation 3-series). In the standard two-volume BMW reference book by Halwart Schrader, there is no mention of the 320i; he quotes a figure of only 14,970 for the 318i; and you look in vain for any mention of the 215bhp version of the M3 convertible model. The figures quoted below, therefore, have been checked in co-operation with the BMW archive.

With the exception of the Baur cabriolet version, no production figures are listed for models in current production, including the most recent 3-series (E36), the M3 and the Z3.

PRODUCTION FIGURES FOR PRE-WAR OPEN BMWs

Model	Body type	Years	Number made
BMW 3/15 DA2	Tourer	1929-31	1834
	Two-seater cabriolet		300
	Four-seater cabriolet		1374
BMW 3/15 DA3	Wartburg: Two-seater roadster	1930-31	150
BMW 3/15 DA4	Tourer	1931-32	175
BMW 3/20 AM1-AM4	Tourer	1932-34	252
	Two-seater cabriolet		11
	Four-seater cabriolet		471
BMW 303	Sports cabriolet	1933-34	27
	Tourer		2
	Four-window cabriolet		542
BMW 309	Tourer	1934-36	179
	Four-window cabriolet		284
BMW 315	Sports cabriolet	1935-37	20
	Tourer		137
	Four-window cabriolet		2281
BMW 315/1	Two-seater roadster		230
BMW 319	Sports cabriolet	1935-37	238
	Tourer		75
	Four-window cabriolet		2066
BMW 319/1	Two-seater roadster		178
BMW 329	Sports cabriolet	1936-37	42
	Four-window cabriolet		1011
BMW 320	Four-window cabriolet	1937-38	1635
BMW 321	Four-window cabriolet	1939-41	1551
BMW 326	Four-window cabriolet	1936-41	4060
	Four-door cabriolet		1093
BMW 327	Sports cabriolet	1937-41	1124
BMW 327/28	Sports cabriolet	1938-40	482
BMW 328	Two-seater roadster (incl. chassis deliveries)	1936-40	461
BMW 335	Two-door cabriolet	1939-41	118
	Four-door cabriolet		40
Grand total			22,443★

★ Excludes chassis with special roadster or cabriolet bodywork.
Source: *Alle BMW-Automobile* by Werner Oswald (English edition: *BMW from 1928 – The Complete Story*, translated and revised by Jeremy Walton)

Annual production of the BMW 328
Chassis numbers from 85001 to 85464:

1936	2
1937	162
1938	158
1939	128
1940	11
Total	461★

★ Includes 59 chassis only deliveries

PRODUCTION FIGURES FOR POST-WAR OPEN BMWs

Model	Body type	Years	Number made
BMW 501/502	Two-door convertible	1954-64	255
	Four-door convertible		65
BMW 503	Convertible	1956-60	138
BMW 507	Two-seater roadster	1955-59	252
BMW 700	Convertible	1959-62	2592
BMW 3200 CS	Convertible	1963	1
BMW 1600-2 (1602)	Full convertible	1967-71	1682
BMW 2002	Full convertible	1971	256
BMW 2002	Baur Targa convertible	1971-75	2272
BMW 3-series E21	Baur Targa convertible	1977-83	4595
BMW 3-series E30	Baur Targa convertible	1983-91	14455
BMW 3-series E30	325i convertible	1986-92	78960
	320i convertible	1986-92	32683
	318i convertible	1990-92	22546
	M3 convertible (200bhp)	1988-91	786
	M3 convertible (215bhp)	1991-93	n/a
BMW Z1	Two-seater roadster	1988-91	8012
BMW 3-series E36	Baur four-door Targa convertible	1992 on	300★
	318i convertible	1993 on	current
	320i convertible	1993 on	current
	328i convertible	1993 on	current
	M3 convertible	1993 on	current
BMW Z3	Two-seater roadster	1995 on	current

★ To the end of 1995

Annual production of the BMW 507
Chassis numbers from 70001 to 70254:

1955	2
1956	1
1957	103
1958	99
1959	47
Total	252★

★ Includes two chassis only deliveries

Annual production of the BMW Z1
Chassis numbers from AL 00000 to Al 08012

1986/87	12
1988	58
1989	2400
1990	4091
1991	1451
Total	8012

ACKNOWLEDGEMENTS

I could not have written and compiled this book without the help of many good friends in the BMW world. Help and advice were generously provided by Hans-Hartmut Krombach of the BMW Veteranen Club Deutschland e.V., Wolfgang Niefanger of the BMW V8 Club, Helmut Feierabend (BMW restoration specialist of Würzburg) and Wolf-D. Gehrmann (BMW expert of Wiesbaden). Particular thanks are due to the staff of BMW's external affairs department and of the BMW Mobile Trandition. These include Alfred Broede, Reinhard Fretschner, Uwe Mahla and Dr Klaus Zwingenberger of the BMW press office, as well as Christian Eich, Dirk-Hennig Strassl and Richard Gerstner from Mobile Tradition. Further information and illustrations came from Maria Wenzelburger of Baur Coachworks in Stuttgart, Jürgen Krein of Wiesmann Motorsport in Dülmen, and Henning Zaiss of the Authenrieth archive in Darmstadt. Last but far from least, I thank Rita Strothjohann, Heinrich Klebl and Peter Zollner of BMW's historical archive for their invaluable assistance in providing not only many of the photographs which appear in this book but also for tirelessly checking production figures and other facts.